A TRILOGY FOR CHRIST

PART TWO

OF PREACHING IN AMERICA

By

TOUMA AL-KHOURY

Edited

By

Archpriest
Michel Najim (PH.D.)

Oakwood Publications

A Trilogy for Christ: Part Two
Of Preaching in America

ALL RIGHTS RESERVED

A TRILOGY FOR CHRIST

PART TWO

OF PREACHING IN AMERICA

PART ONE

ORTHODOX FATHERS, ORTHODOX FAITH
(Available)

PART THREE

THE CONTEMPLATIONS OF JUDAS ISCARIOT

(Available October, 1995)

A TRILOGY FOR CHRIST

PART TWO

OF PREACHING IN AMERICA

"Use what you have learned to have an impact upon your community, your state, and your nation."

John Eldsmon
(God and Caesar: The Epilogue)

"Christians should be involved in debating the great issues of our time."

William J. Bennett
(From his Foreword to: Politically Incorrect: By Ralph Reed.)

CONTENTS

I

A Free Forum   for the Distorting of the Scriptures and the Sacrilege of the Sacred Alike

Prelude

Modern day preaching in America has indeed fallen on hard times. Most of it seems to be bad news rather than the good news of the Gospel - bad news because it mixes scripture with modern day philosophy and psychology. This mixture is "bad" inasmuch as such a mix <u>cannot</u> save modern man from the stress and self-serving love of modern day life, and deliver him safe and sound into the kingdom of Heaven.

Mr. Touma Al-Khoury has in a very excellent and straightforward manner analyzed this "mix," separated the wheat from the chaff of bad thinking and manners, and presented a call for return to the true Christian faith. Such a return would be good for America, for it would bring true healing to its citizenry and produce the kind of citizens that truly love God, Church and country.

Archpriest Richard Ballew
Sacramento, CA

INTRODUCTION

The East is generally viewed by Americans as somewhat mysterious, if not outright incomprehensible. This is an amazing situation since Americans by and large consider themselves Christian, and Christianity is basically an Eastern religion. It is this little understood Eastern perspective which Touma Al-Khoury, from the Syrian church of Antioch (Oriental Orthodox), brings to his "Trilogy for Christ." In *Of Preaching in America*, his second book of the Trilogy, Al-Khoury has examined the multifarious nature of Protestantism in America and is compelled to express his gut reaction to it. Little escapes his analytical eye: From Mormonism and the Jehovah's Witnesses to Robert Schuller, from apocalyptic dispensationalists like John Walvoord to unbelieving "bishops" like John Sponge, Al-Khoury here encompasses most of what is implied by the umbrella term "American Christianity."

In his uncomplicated directness, Touma Al-Khoury is indeed a modern apostle in whom there is no guile (cf. John 1:47). His candid and simple assessments of the "gospels" preached in America, whether it be the gospel of fundamentalist millenarianism or the psychobabble of the "feel good" self-esteem religion, will resonate with the average American reader. We are familiar with the religious proclivities which Al-Khoury observes and are struck by how much they differ from the ancient Faith of the Near East which he represents. In a sense, Al-Khoury is a missionary calling Americans away from their incessant religious fads and back to the biblical Gospel which has been followed by the Christians of the Near East for two thousand years. In an interesting twist on this evangelistic theme, *Of Preaching in America* starts with an autobiographical anecdote entitled "Born Again" which recounts how Al-Khoury, as a young man in Lebanon, met an American missionary who was in reality a wolf stalking Christ's sheep, proselytizing Eastern Christians out of their Faith through confrontation and intimidation. The rest of the book subtly suggests that, rather than sending missionaries abroad, America ought to be receiving them from those who are more mature in the Gospel than she.

But Al-Khoury's message must not be misconstrued as being merely negative or as just narrow polemics. On the contrary, Al-Khoury is not any less reserved in his eagerness to dialogue with other confessions than he is to critique American pop spirituality, which critiques ought to be understood in the light of his expansive openness to what is positive in American Christianity. He is convinced that the Holy Spirit can be found wherever there are honest people who sincerely seek Him (cf. Matthew 7:8), and in the presence of the Holy Spirit there is no place for obtuse reproaches and recriminations. Thus Touma Al-Khoury's sometimes pointed commentary is intended to be constructive in nature, as sage counsel drawn from the Syrian Christian tradition in which Al-Khoury joyously revels like a young man with a new bride.

Though Al-Khoury normally writes in a clear and straightforward fashion, English obviously isn't his first language and he occasionally phrases things in an innovative manner. Yet, surprisingly, even his unique parlance seems to work as a fitting vehicle for his unique insights. His overall style is what might be described, in the particularly American connotation of the word, as "evangelical." Rather than tedious erudition, Al-Khoury prefers a simple appeal to the New Testament and common sense.

In this and other respects the book is tailor-made for its American audience, and many of the sentiments which Al-Khoury articulates echo those which Americans themselves frequently express. In pondering the awesome salaries of American televangelists, Al-Khoury can only register his incredulity and wonder whether any of these self-proclaimed ministers of the word of God have ever stumbled across Jesus' words, "Verily I say unto you, That a rich man shall hardly enter into the kingdom of heaven" (Matthew 19:23). With similar forthrightness, Al-Khoury expresses amazement at a 1991 Supreme Court decision which, by a slim 5-4 majority, upheld a public decency law in South Bend, Indiana requiring nude dancers in night clubs to at least wear panties and G-strings. The court's thinking was that while nude dancing was a form of free speech entitled to a measure of protection by the First Amendment, the states may ban it in the interest of protecting public order and morality. Al-Khoury doesn't miss the irony of "public order and morality" in America hanging by a G-string. He bluntly proposes to his readers that, if American society is incapable of seeing that there is no moral difference between "nude dancing" and dancing with "panties and a G-string," the fault lies with America's religious leaders who are more interested in pleasing their listeners than preaching the Gospel. While on the surface such rebukes of the clergy may sound harsh, still we recognize that they are ones which have frequently been made by Americans themselves; indeed, they are even frequently made by

American clergy from the pulpit, though it is more often a criticism leveled at another preacher than a serious self-examination of conscience.

It should be noted, however, that this book isn't only for the reader born and raised in the United States; it will also be much appreciated by the newly arrived immigrant. America has a distinctive spiritual milieu which can only be likened to a stew of many different religious beliefs; and the Christian who immigrates to this country can easily become confused, overwhelmed and finally sucked into one of the innumerable sects. As an example of this, one need only look at the famous televangelist of the quintessentially American name-it-and-claim-it "Health and Wealth Gospel," Benny Hinn. Benny was baptized by the Eastern Orthodox Patriarch of Jerusalem, Benedictus, after whom he was named during the ceremony. He immigrated to Toronto with his family from Jaffa, Palestine (where his father was once the mayor), and was quickly swept up into the charismatic movement at a Kathryn Khulman healing revival in Pittsburgh. He shortly afterwards began preaching at a little pentecostal church, working ceaselessly -- and in the end successfully -- to convert the rest of his family. The attitude Benny Hinn has adopted toward his Eastern Christian heritage can be gleaned from his description of his own mother, Clemence Hinn, before her conversion to pentecostalism as "a devout Greek Orthodox woman, but she didn't know much about the Lord." By surveying and critiquing the American spiritual landscape, Touma Al-Khoury has rendered a great service to all the possible Benny Hinns of the future. His work leaves the reader with no doubt that to be a "devout" Eastern Christian means to know the Lord in the fullest possible sense.

I am excited that the reading public in America is being introduced to a new (yet ancient) aspect of Christianity. When reading this book, put aside any thought of highlighting or taking notes; this is not so much a book to be studied as it is one to be savored and enjoyed. It is a compelling book, powerful without being ponderous. Therefore I recommend a quiet evening, a comfortable couch, a good reading lamp and an old pair of slippers. If you're like I was, you won't greet the dawn before having turned the last page.

T.L. Frazier

January 29, 1995

Feast of the Relics of St Ignatius of Antioch.

PROLOGUE

BORN AGAIN

In the first week of my permanent residence in America, a relative came to visit me and said, "If the Buddhist reincarnation or metempsychosis was a true doctrine, then the preacher you portrayed long ago in one of your short stories entitled 'Born Again,' seems to have been reborn in another pastor here in America. We could watch him next week together on TV."

I watched him that very week and many weeks thereafter attacking with his incendiary style, sin, sexual immoralities, pornography, Communism, Catholicism, Jews and fellow Protestants as well.

Yes, many times I watched this dynamic and fiery preacher Jimmy Swaggart, swaggering and strutting on the stage from side to side, brandishing his Bible aloft in one hand, gesticulating, shouting, weeping and making others weep.

As to my dismay and astonishment, I also watched his sudden and saddening fall, ensuing his scandal, his sexual indiscretions that were unfolded on February 18, 1988.

It seems that like the scribes and Pharisees of old, Jimmy Swaggart used to preach and teach; whereas he himself didn't do and behave accordingly.[1]

Nevertheless, nobody has the right to judge him. Who are we to judge another's servant?[2] I personally do believe sincerely in believers through his preaching; and they must be many (if they will persist and persevere in their firm faith in Christ as their God and sole Savior, and keep constantly his commandments).

Furthermore, long before being on TV, Jimmy Swaggart had also preached on radio, "opened mission and charity offices in 53 countries and (preached) regularly overseas", as reports Time magazine, February 17, 1986.

---

[1]-*(Matthew 23:3).*

[2]-*(Romans 14:4).*

When Jesus' disciples forbade someone once not following them, because of casting demons in Christ's name, Jesus rebuked them saying, "Do no forbid him for he who is not against us is on our side,[3] or "is for us."[4]

Both good and false preachers of the Gospel, sooner or later will be discovered, "For there is nothing covered that will not be revealed, and hidden that will not be known."[5] They will be, thus, revealed through their very conduct and behavior, through their works and deeds indeed. As Christ Jesus asserted "you will know them by their fruits."[6]

Therefore, I found it convenient, rather useful to introduce this second book of mine in English, "Of Preaching In America" by that same short story I published in Arabic almost thirty years ago under the title Born Again, so that "He who has ears to hear, let him hear."[7]

---

[3]-(Mark 9:38-40)

[4]-(Luke 9:50)

[5]-(Matthew 10:26 and Mark 4:22 and Luke 8:17)

[6]-(Matthew 7:16 and Luke 6:45)

[7]-(Matthew 13:9)

And here is that short story that I
translated into English and modified slightly.

BORN AGAIN[1]

I was just about to have my dinner, when my friend Isaiah burst in panting. And without saluting, he said: "Follow me at once. There is a prodigious preacher who animates stones. . . transforms sinners into saints. People by hundreds, by thousands, from different denominations, are pouring to him. Tonight he will deliver his last sermon. . . Believe me, the very preacher you would really like."

Isaiah was quite aware of my negative attitude with regard to such evangelists, to whom my father (a priest also) used to say while arguing with them, "The eighth commandment does state, "you shall not steal." Why then are you robbing stones from our church? Go to the quarries nearby. They are full of stones, brand new stones, and build with your churches." Because, in fact, in the vicinity

[1]-Published first in Al-Nour-the light--an Orthodox magazine of the Orthodox youth movement in Beirut Lebanon, 1962.

1

along the rocky coast there were a lot of quarries. By "new stones" my father meant Moslems populating the whole area to whom those evangelists dared not to preach. They were rather endeavoring to convert the faithful among other congregations and denominations to their own sect. And my father added, "Besides, by preaching Christians, you are contradicting even Paul who says, "Thus I have made it my aim to preach the gospel, not where Christ has already been named, so that I do not build on someone else's foundation."[2]

"I am afraid of not finding vacant places in the church," Isaiah continued after breathing a sigh of relief. "The taxi driver is already waiting for us."

And he stepped out. To her dismay, noticing me following my friend without having dinner yet, my wife, agape, stood still at the door unable to utter a single word. Maybe she talked to me while descending the stairs frantically after him, but I didn't hear her. I was still stunned by Isaiah's words, "A prodigious preacher that animates stones, and transforms sinners into saints. The very type you would really like."

---

[2]-(Romans 15:20)

True, neither a great sinner I was nor a saint whom angels envied. I was rather in between so to speak. For I had shortcomings that I was ashamed of, and virtues I used to brag about or refrain from disclosing in due time. Besides, I was very eager to attend religious meetings and listen to subjects that dealt with good and evil, heaven and hell, angels and sinners, death and resurrection and the like; namely the metaphysical problems that perplex both mind and imagination, and around which opinions are most often diverse and divisive, controversial and contradictory. Besides you are always teetering between firm faith and deceiving doubt that arouse your curiosity to listen to again and again.

As for my interest in all those matters, it all started when I was a child; when I used to listen constantly to a noted neighbor so witty and versed in the Scriptures that his home was always full of curious people like me. Oh, how often I neglected my homework and gathered there to listen anxiously to their stormy debates with him. So, being late, my mother, without hailing, used to storm in, snatching my arm and dragging me among their laughters.

As Isaiah had already expected, the Church was packed full with people of different denominations. The standees in the aisles

3

seemed to outnumber those in the pews. Perhaps because of my tall stature and white suit, and the black garment of my short companion who looked like a clergyman, a young gentleman approached us with a very polite manner, and invited both of us to follow him. To our astonishment, he ushered us to the first row in the foreground just below the pulpit, where distinguished persons were sitting on luxurious armchairs. What embarrassed me the most was being the focus of attention. I couldn't even avoid the master of ceremony on the stage who, while advancing to the pulpit, did welcome me with a slight smile. Ashamed, I nodded to him, stooped and followed the usher. But no sooner was I seated to the left of an elderly woman, then I noticed again the master of ceremony still following us with his eyes, making sure that we had reached our destination so that he could begin his speech. Isaiah in turn, while looking hurriedly for his seat next to me, bumped the foot of a respectable young lady at his left. He apologized mumbling in a funny way. Whereas the man sitting beside the woman, her husband maybe, frowned without uttering a word.

After introducing the Preacher with terse terms lacking not humble praise and vivid plaudits, the master of ceremony retired in the same swift way he entered the scene. Behold, the door behind the stage opened, and a burly and brown man, very brown, with short hair almost shaved, entered and stepped towards the pulpit with hasty but steady pace.

"This is the Preacher" whispered Isaiah in my ear. He was as I said dark brown, and good looking; He had a sound and strong constitution. I noticed his large barrel chest dominating the pulpit, and his hand grasping the sides of the platform with fat and forceful fingers like a pair of pincers. He was wearing a dark black suit which increased his browness, except for his snow white shirt and collar, so that as two straight lines between the red necktie and the vest, were joining in a big V, ending with the single button of his jacket. And above this whiteness and browness spread all over with a showy elegance, a pair of dark eyes from which quick and pierce glances shot through his eye glasses.

The preacher stood still for a few moments, staring at his large audience, calmly and vigilantly, as if waiting for total silence to permeate the souls, for ears to be more attentive, and hearts more receptive to his sermon.

Then he opened his mouth and spoke. By symbols he talked and by allegories, precepts and parables. He spoke with a sonorous sounding and splendid voice, modulating from profound and powerful to soft and sweet. From his grandiloquence and language, so fluent and fluid, I attested that he was long since a professor of literature. Because of his nebulous and diaphanous style adorned with metaphors and analogies, he seemed to be a real poet. Nay, because he never ceased prowling and parading on the stage, with such easiness and alertness, elegance and grace, gesticulating and gesturing, I attested to Isaiah betting that he practiced being on stage, either as a real actor or orator before being a pastor.

Thus, encouraged by the delight and astonishment of his auditors so that you could literally hear the pounding of their hearts, he persevered to the utmost his performance, his stylistic oration, as if words were heavenly inspired. He was really an actor, orator, raconteur, poet and priest altogether. His sermon was a masterpiece, a marvelous mixture of Demosthene's declaration and Chrysostom's eloquence. I was really awestruck by his performance and magniloquence more than his spiritual sermon.

When he stopped awhile as to take a break for the first time, we didn't expect him to deliver more than he did. Then to our astonishment, he proceeded and presented his unprecedented and unpredictable parable. He said, talking now about another preacher, a Western one (that he named but I forget the name); and playing his role on the stage at the same time:

"The preacher, he said: was on his stage, like me now, but outside, in the large open square of the Nation's Capital. While the multitudes were listening to him sermonizing, the pavement of the street trembled under the footfall of horses' hooves. And lo, a magnificent chariot adorned with gold and ivory appeared; then approached with pomp and splendor the preacher's pulpit. It was drawn by six superbly beautiful and thoroughbred horses whose muscles were moving under a polished, smooth and splendid skin. Thousands of eyes were staring at the chariot. The preacher and the mob recognized it. It was the queen's chariot. People suffered too much because of her oppression and reluctantly disregarded her dissoluteness and debauchery.

"Then the preacher turned around, stretched his long arm as a palm branch towards the queen, shouting with vim and vigor:

"Country men, here is the tyrant Jezebel. Here is your queen."

"Hearing his terrible terms, the queen pulled the chariot's curtain, and her eyes were about to wink because of his fingers were still like a spearhead wagging at her in a menacing manner. Here the preacher, addressing the mob, shouted in a ringing and resonant voice saying:
"Who would buy the Queen? Yes, who would purchase the precious Queen?"

It was indeed a queer question that shocked and shook the multitude as a whirlwind. A mare neighed as a protest against the abominable insolence of the preacher who persisted and repeated with more vehement tone, pointing again to the cowardly Queen:

"Who among you good citizens, is willing to buy the Queen, I said?"

"A tense silence fell over the crowds. Heads bowed, and statures collapsed, as if every individual was personally accountable rather culpable because of the contemptuous question requested time and again.

Playing always the role of both the alleged seller and buyer, the preacher continued.

"I would buy her."

"Who are you arrogant creature to dare to buy our great Queen"?

"I am Money. I am Mammon. I am the Lord of the World."

"No, no money or mammon of the entire world can buy even the sandal strap of our priceless Queen."

And here, a wave of ease did permeate the multitudes who were about to heave a sign of relief, when suddenly the voice of the preacher shouted vehemently:

"Who among you is really capable of buying our Queen?"

"I am; preacher. Yes, indeed, I would purchase the Queen."

"You? But who are you daredevil stranger?"

"I am he who in worship to me, heads bow. I am he who at my door, knees prostrate, bodies bend, and souls melt. I am Glory and Fame, Splendor and Sublimity."

"Absurdity. Nonsense. Ha, ha, ha".

"How are you mocking me miserable preacher. I said I would buy her indeed."

"And I say, presumptuous purchaser, that no gold or glory of the whole world is worth even the nails clippings of our Great and Glorious Queen."

There was anew an audible sigh of relief and laughter among the joyous throng. But at this very moment, a troop of armed forces on horses stormed and surrounded the place. Surprised and scared to death were the populace. Whereas the preacher, even without blinking, resumed his daring question. Nay, his voice now was expressly more firm and fomenting, more strong and sarcastic as to scratch the ears of the soldiers themselves.

"Who among you, guardians of the country would dare purchase our Queen? No one? Alas."

With authoritative glance and wave of her hand, the Queen silenced the rattling of sabers in their scabbards.

And the preacher went on to leap, gesticulate, prowl the stage and ask frantically.

"Neither you handsome officer of the guard? Nor you old man there? Look at your Queen. She is as gorgeous as a goddess."

Again, uncanny silence was about to stir and spur the soldiers, lest the voice of the preacher rang now, with unusual questions and answers, changing from burst to broken, from thunder to tender, and whisper.

"Peace with you piteous preacher. I bought the Queen."

"You said what, stranger!?"

"I said, I already purchased her. The Queen is mine now, under my own dominion, in my private possession."

"I can't believe it. I can't believe it. But in exchange of what did you buy her?"

"Of course, not with material things like silver, gold or glory, but by my own gore that was shed on Calvary. By my precious blood I purchased the Queen."

"Oh gracious God! Oh sweet Jesus! No. There is no greater love, greater sacrifice than yours. In whom we take refuge than in you? You are the way, you are the truth, and you are the life. Amen."

And here, the church exploded with thunderous ovations as if it was torpedoed by tons of dynamite. A charge of electric ecstasy seized the souls, and pervaded the hearts like catharsis in the tragedies of the Ancient Greek great poets, Eschylos, Sophoclis and Euripides.

Depicting the last scene in his parable, our prodigious preacher said, "The solemn silence that seized masses in that great open square of the capital, was interrupted for the second time, by the neigh of a horse that began to strike the floor by iron hooves, emitting sparks, as if they were striking the inner most of the Queen's heart, and setting it on intense fire and flame. Ashamed to death, the Queen nodded, retreated with her troops, weeping, repenting and returning to Lord Christ and Savior. And the mob rejoiced at her sight, and the sight of tears welling in the preacher's eyes, and flowing out, filling his palms. His uncovered face was now so radiant, so glowing, as if illuminated by the blessings of heaven."

Again a splendid ovation was heard in the church.

"Great, wasn't he?" repeated Isaiah whispering to me.

"Wonderful! Really wonderful!" I said muttering.

"Didn't I tell you?"

Paying no more heed to Isaiah's repeated remarks and praise about the preacher, I pondered: On one hand, I marveled at Christ's great love and sacrifice for mankind; and saw in Him alone, as I have always seen, the Supreme God that surpassed even as a historical man and Son of Man, all other gods. Nay, I saw no one else but Him, as the sole, single, and unique God of our planet earth that is sinking perpetually in its constant worries and concerns, troubles and turmoils, dreads and dilemmas. On the other hand, I admired this prodigious preacher, still standing on the stage, with his graceful and good looks, so delighted to the delight and joy of his audience, savoring leisurely their great felicity. I equally marvelled at the wit of the western preacher who through his peculiar and profound parable, could convert a straying Queen.

Now, when the audience was about to leave the church, it was the master of ceremony who stopped them by a gentle gesture of his both hands. And they sat down, watching gladly the preacher and the master of ceremony, awaiting impatiently the new pending surprise. In that very solemn evening we were expecting many wonders, even the opening of the sky and the landing of angels on earth. For people everywhere are so thirsty and hungry for the very Word of God, so that they are ready to hear it restlessly all their lifetime.

And lo, the preacher, accompanied by the master of ceremony, descended the stage and marched calmly towards those sitting in the front, always grinning and waving. It seemed to me he was asking them questions, but I couldn't hear him because he was still at the far side of the front line. As every time he was passing from one person to another, eyes were focussing on him and attentive ears were yearning to catch what he was saying.

In the meantime, while still absorbed in evaluating his skill in sounding the social consciences, and captivating by his eloquence, the minds of the crowd, behold my ears perked up.

"Are you born again"?

So this was his question every time he passed from one person to another, I said within myself, when furtively and stealthily he approached the old woman sitting next to me. She was a middle-aged woman shabbily, but properly dressed; and presumably from a middle-class background.

"I am asking you, if you are born again Madam?"

Confused, she began to teeter and stammer, knowing not how exactly to respond to him. This was the first time she was hearing such a question. (For in our churches in the Middle East, preachers or pastors don't ask the faithful such a question).

Thinking she was somehow deaf, the preacher stooped and asked her loudly, "I am asking you if you are now born again?"

Moving uneasily in her seat, the old woman eyed him silently for a while; and again she mumbled and trembled saying, "Truly...I don't know. . . what. . . what to say . . . exactly."

15

"Ah," exclaimed the preacher, "It seems to me that you are afraid to say what really is on your mind. . . Although my question is very simple."

"I know. . . I know . . . but you know" she uttered hesitantly, and taking off, this time, her eye glasses.

And here the preacher bent forward, and down, and asked her with a tart tone revealing discomfort and discontent as if he was fed up with her.

"I asked you Madam if you have been born again after my speech. Answer my question: yes or no?"

"Oh yes, yes. . . but. . . but I have still a hazy idea about. . . about" she said in such a hurried and weepy way that I felt sorry for her.

"But about what?" asked the preacher sharply, and shaking his hand in front of her. Then with a harsh voice and warning;

"Look at me Madam. Do you know what does Jesus say?"

"No", she answered hastily and always hesitatingly.

"He says word for word, "For whoever is ashamed of me and my words in this adulterous and sinful generation of Him the Son of Man also will be ashamed." And he pronounced his last sentence with such a majestic tone of voice that sent a shocking tumult and murmur through the whole audience.

Trembling before him as before God's throne, the woman moaned and cried,

"Oh no. . no. No I am not ashamed of Christ."

"Oh yes Madam; and the proof is that you are ashamed to testify that you are born again, and you are trembling."

"But no. . no."

"But yes, yes," he interrupted her abruptly, "Long before you, Peter denied Christ thrice."

The woman was about to faint. And a heavy silence fell on the church for a few moments. Turning all this over in my mind, I was now quite aware of all the preacher's tricks and tactics. I felt an urge to expose him openly.

17

"Your preacher is exaggerating," I whispered to Isaiah. "He has infuriated the whole audience."

"In fact he. . ." and smiled without continuing his phrase.

And the preacher repeated vehemently, "Yes, three times."

And the woman tried to defend herself, "But sir."

Without giving her a respite, he continued, "Yes indeed, tomorrow you will meet your neighbor and she will ask you, "Have you really been in that church? And have you listened to that preacher? And of course, he has converted you, and certainly you have been born again."

"No, no," she desperately whimpered in protest.

Turning his back halfway to her, seeming not to notice her protest, he continued, addressing now the audience as with a fresh, new sermon, "Says the Lord, be cold or hot. But do not be lukewarm lest I will spew you out of my mouth."

And while explaining this saying of the Lord, I began to ponder afresh the preacher's sly and skillful game. He is certainly a genius psychologist. He mercilessly trapped her in his snare as he did with many others. He is like all other preachers, predators of easy prey. His sole purpose is to convert her to his own sect. The saying of the Lord "Whoever is ashamed of me... I also will be ashamed of him, etc." will ring in her ears... And my ears perked up anew at:

"Are you, Sir, a born again?"

I wasn't aware that the question was addressed to me now, when Isaiah tapped twice my shoulder and said to me, "The reverend preacher is asking you."

And the preacher, interrupted my friend, and said to me, "I am asking, Sir, if you have been born again today?"

At that very moment I regained full consciousness. The preacher was still standing next to me with his pale, pitiful face and empty eyes as if he was asking me alms and charity. And I didn't feel pity for him. Rather, I winced, leaned back in my comfortable seat and seeking more relaxation, I started to scan and size him up carefully. And a slight smile disappeared quickly as it appeared at the left corner of his lips, as if he was disgusted with his ceaseless, monotonous, and automatic question addressed to Christians that are maybe more genuine, more faithful than him.

Then an unbidden answer rose to my lips and said, "Oh. As for me. . . most reverend preacher and teacher of the Gospel, (then very quietly, purposely, and punctiliously) Oh. Yes, as for me, even before having the great honor... to listen to your outstanding... very stupendous. .. and sensational sermon, yes, I am, and . . ."

As aware now of my tricky response, he didn't let me continue my sentence. He dashed forward as if leaping over a large gap. But my quick words dashed through and jumped after him jerking and jolting his ears, "and, yes I am still, as I have always been, keeping in Christ a new creation."

"What was your response to him sir?" asked me the old woman sitting beside me. "It seems he didn't stop too long with you."

Her countenance was so sad and broken with great affliction. I felt sorry for her for the second time, and said, "I said to him that I was always a new creation in Christ even before hearing his sermon."

"Alas!" she uttered literally and receded frightened, her hand clutching convulsively her dress on the chest as if to suppress a shiver.

"What is the matter with you Madam?" I said smiling.

"Nothing. . . Nothing. . .Your response to him was better than mine."

Feigning that I was unaware of her response to him, and not mindful of those long sardonic and menacing words of the preacher to her, I said, "By the way, what was your reply to him?"

She looked all around escaping the eyes of those around her and as if she was confessing a great sin or revealing a significant secret, she murmured, "I think. . . I think I said something similar. . . but, but I don't know, I don't remember well."

"If so, what is wrong with that Madam? Don't worry. Don't you believe in Christ as your God and sole Savior?"

"Of course I do. Certainly I do love Him and worship Him constantly. The crucifix is over my bed. Day and night I pray to Christ to deliver me from evil and forgive all my sins".

"But why are you then so confused? Do you feel guilty of something you said wrong? To the preacher, for example"?

"Not exactly. . . maybe. . . I don't know" she said calmly and kept wiping unseen dust off her black purse on her lap.

I couldn't refrain from laughing because of her frankness and naiveness. And to tease her a bit, I said imitating the menacing tone of the preacher, "Don't forget Madam. Do you know what Jesus said? For whoever is ashamed of Me and My words, of him the Son of Man also will be ashamed."

"So you heard our conversation?" she interrupted me.

"I heard it verbatim Madam; and you were very sincere, very frank and brave with you responses to the preacher, because for the first time you were hearing such an expression "are you born again?"

"Yes indeed. Thank you so much," and ashamed, she bowed her head smiling as being totally relieved this time.

And I began to watch the predator preacher now out of sight, forcing his way among the throng and performing his lucrative hunting.

Back home, Isaiah asked me;

"Tell me, are you now born again?"

"Didn't you hear my response to the preacher?"

"Frankly, no. Because I was in turn busy preparing myself to his question as to my exact response to him."

"Very good, Isaiah. So have you been born again today?"

"Yes, of course."

"I say today."

"Yes indeed. I swear by God."

"Don't swear", say the Scriptures. What about tomorrow, and the day after tomorrow? And what about the next year, and the years to come, Isaiah?"

"I don't understand you."

"The juggler who does his performance, displays his many tricks in the middle of squares and open roads, have you never seen him?"

"What is the matter with him?"

"He might bite and gnaw stones, eat glass, swallow up blaze, swallow a cubit of an iron bar."

"And so on and so forth, and what else?"

"This swindler, or juggler, or trickster might startle, astonish, distract, and disturb me. But believe me Isaiah, he will never, ever deceive me or confuse me."

And my friend burst in a bitter laughter and said, "You mean the preacher?"

"I mean", I interrupted him, "even liars can talk abundantly about truth and convince people; even the corrupt, the deceitful, the hypocrite can preach about righteousness, virtue, decency, gallantry and excel, and surpass, and marvel people. But all of them, Isaiah, you shall know them by their fruits. And perhaps, I guess, you yourself have watched this evening the harvest with your own eyes."

"Do you mean his answers to the old woman?"

"I mean his cruel way intimidating the poor and naive woman."

"But don't you agree with me that he was quite right, although he exaggerated a bit, maybe on purpose too?"

"You are smart, Isaiah, even though you feign sometimes to play the hypocrite, of course as a matter of joking. At any rate, I didn't lose my dinner tonight."

A DARING DEDICATION

Before being the land of science and cinema, opportunities and peculiarities, creation and innovation, America has always been to me, the fantastic feat of all times. Namely, the most powerful and bountiful country made out of fifty feeble and somehow squabbling states, as the miraculous and glorious Nation formed of diverse and different nations and nationalities.

Moreover, to me, America was the very logos that abolished for the first time the very myth, so to speak, of the Tower of Babel. For in spite of her various and numerous languages, one "pure language" i.e. the English language, unified her; and is about to unify the whole world, fulfilling thereby somehow Zephenia's prophecy, "For then I will restore to the peoples nearly a pure language, that they all may call on the name of the Lord, to serve him with one accord."[10] [About the desire to learn

---

[10]- *(Zephenia 3:9)*

the "dominant languages of the world-naturally English" San Francisco Examiner, Sunday February 19, 1995 reports that Michael Krauss, a language researcher at the university of Alaska said: Between 20 and 50% of the world's languages are no longer being learned by children. "For the next century, something up to 95% of mankind's languages will either become extinct or become moribund and headed toward extinction."]

Even though her sky scrapers' tops are in heaven, and her Man on the Moon, the message that Buzz Aldrin relayed to planet Earth on July 1969, was David's psalm glorifying God in creation:

When I look at your heavens, the work of your fingers,
The moon and the stars, that you have established,
What is man that you are mindful of him,
And the son of man that you care for him?[11]

[A direct or indirect allusion maybe to Nikita Khroutchev's ironic and boastful bragging that they, the Communists, "did not

---

[11]-(Psalm 8:3,4)

see God" when they launched Sputnik, the first earth satellite on October 1957.]

America also was to me the Mesoceania of the most recent and resplendent of all civilizations that crowned Mesopotamia, the very Cradle of Civilization that brought forth monotheism, the plow, the law, the alphabet, the wheel, and the ziggurat or the protopyramid par excellence.

However, the first four years I lived in America, I was really bewildered, rather staggered, by another fabulous phenomenon utterly unknown to me before, namely the captivating act of preaching and teaching the Gospel day and night, through all sorts of the most modernized media. Even in the very youth and beginning of Christianity, this cosmic event in the history of humankind was not so in vogue, vigor, and vitality as I noticed it in America. Time Magazine, February 17, 1986, put it this way, "Broadcasting's Jesus network comprises 200 local TV stations that have religious formats (more than double the figure a year ago), 1,134 radio stations (up 91 from last year), free lance productions that purchase time on general stations, and burgeoning cable and satellite hookups that reach tens of millions of homes. . . According to a 1977 estimate by Television/Radio Age, $500 millions were spent to purchase TV and radio time a decade ago; today Armstrong figures the total is $1 billion, possibly $2 billion. That does not count other expenses and the ambitious ancillary enterprises that must have launched."

Hence, I would like to dedicate this second book of mine in English, entitled "Of Preaching In America," to some particular and prominent preachers and teachers of the Gospel in America (But not without reserve, reproach, and severe criticism) sparing no one save TRUTH; nay, naming each by his proper name, and combatting, always in the light of the Scriptures themselves, some of their deviations and strange doctrines.

Yes, I am gladly dedicating it especially to these dynamic pastor-orators of radio, television, pulpit, and principally on podia, rostra and stadia, that remind me of pioneer prophets of old who preached the Word of God as far and forceful as their faith and fortune took them. For among them there are indeed, those who, despite their frailties, faults and fallacies, "in whom there is no guile," as the most humble, the most zealous, the most eloquent, and the most versed in the Scriptures.

Besides, no, nobody can deny or negate the great and bountiful benefits of this cyclic and ceaseless act of preaching, teaching, and propagating of the Gospel that pertain almost, always, and exclusively to Protestantism.

I, personally, testify that through the possessing of a copy of Saint John's Gospel (in Arabic) distributed gratis by a Protestant missionary (that I once read at the age of twenty in a remote and secluded grove) I discovered Jesus Christ's divinity. I endeavored thereafter to invite and encourage others, be they friends or foes, to believe in Him as their only God and sole Savior.

Moreover, how marvelous and miraculous is this blessing of transmitting the Word of God to the elderly, the very young, the infirm, the imprisoned, the handicap, the secular and the heathen, as well as to all those living in remote areas in countless countries of the vast world. This exclusive achievement also, seems to belong somehow particularly to the powerful Protestant missionaries.

No, I don't underestimate the very cost and conveniences of broadcasting and especially of telecasting the Gospel. Says Richard N. Ostling, about "Evangelical Publishing and Broadcasting", "the other most common mainline complaint about TV evangelism concerns the constant pleas of money. TV has a voracious appetite for funds, and it takes huge amounts to produce shows and buy time to put them on the air."[12]

Even though real conversion through modern media is somewhat inconsistent, and their very effect is most often restricted to the faithful; yet, this magnificent and magnanimous feat of diffusing the Word of God through means of mass communications on radios, televisions, movies, cassettes, books, booklets, pamphlets, and many varieties of devices, is also ascribed particularly to these dynamic and genuine Protestant pastors and evangelists who are faithfully preaching the Gospel "to all nations"[13] according to Christ's will.

Now, although the very purpose of most of these preachers and teachers of the Gospel is not my dire and direct concern, yet as an ardent reader, since my youth, of the Bible and other religious cults and cultures and lately, in America, as a fervid listener to radio, and watcher of television when their sermons and

---

[12]-*Evangelicalism and Modern America, Edited by George Marsden, William B. Eerdmuns Publishing Company, Grand Rapids, Michigan. Copyright 1989. Page 51.*

[13]-*(Mark 13:10)*

speeches are broadcast; and as a very devourer of their diverse publications, books, pamphlets, casual articles in newspapers and magazines, and even private letters, I can't help but ask:

Are they indeed as a majority the very violent who take away the Kingdom of heaven by force, according to Matthew 11:12?

Or are they competing to erect their own earthly kingdoms handed down from fathers to sons to grandsons?

On behalf of Christ Jesus are they laboriously working and tenaciously toiling day and night? Or for the sake of Mammon, self-esteem, luxury, and fame, are they in fact striving and struggling constantly?

Because, this very act of preaching and teaching the Gospel in America, as it seems to me, has become again i.e., on a massive scale, almost the right of every single individual regardless of his degree of education, maturity, and basic knowledge in the realm of religion and theology.

In my youth, I was in the habit of attending religious meetings anywhere are available: in churches, clubs, circles, homes, halls and salons. Hence, once in one of these meetings in a private villa in my neighborhood, after reading silently chapter seven, verses fourteen through twenty-five of Paul's epistle to the Romans, each one, in turn, began to explain it and comment on it in his own way. We were more than thirty men and women, old and young, most of them nearly illiterate, in a large and luxurious living room. Everyone had his copy of the New Testament distributed in advance by our host and his wife. But amazingly enough, everyone of the first ten people who had read silently that paragraph, not only gave a false and different interpretation of it, but even the most ridiculous, absurd, and nonsensical as well. To my dismay and great anger, I furiously closed the book when my turn came, stood up, and made, at first, a short sarcastic and didactic speech saying, "knowing only but few cliché verses of the Bible, some may dare discourse and discuss with you for hours even about the most delicate mysteries of Religion. Some others, the ungodly ones, of course, will never ever comprehend the sacred secrets, sense, and spirit of the Scriptures; because, as says David, "The secret of the Lord is with those who fear him."[14] Whereas the third category, the worst in my estimation, includes the majority of people who do attend religious meetings and carry out discussions, only, sad to

---

[14]-(Psalm 25:14)

say, for distraction and digestion of the heavy meals they have been stuffed with." (Here a hilarious laughter in the audience interrupted me). Then, solemnly and severely I continued saying, "Jesus did promise that "Where two or three are gathered together in (his) name (he is) there in the midst of them."[15] But, sad to say again, Satan personally is present now in the midst of us, we, who in the name of Christ, are supposed to be gathered this evening here, in this house. Simply because, not a single person among all those who commented on this paragraph of St Paul's epistle, comprehended its real meaning." And I began to count them expressly one by one to confound them, and got out frantically.

It is Martin Luther himself, the german leader of the Reforamtion (1483-1546) who, "in the early days of his rebellion proclaimed the right of every individual to interpret the Scriptures for himself."[16]

Then almost three hundred years later, Thomas Jefferson (1743-1826), the very drafter

---

[15]-*(Matthew 18:20)*

[16]-*The Story of Civilization, by Will Durant, Simon and Schuster. New York 1957 (Part 6. The Reformation: The Reformation In Germany. P. 370.*

of the declaration of Independence (1755-6) made things worse in matter of religion, when in his "Notes on the State of Virginia," declared that, "...all men shall be free to profess, and by arguments, to maintain their opinion in matters of religion."[17]

Thus, both Luther and Jefferson opened the way wide to many, many "men" or "individuals," rather to a ceaseless series of pseudo-theologians clergymen, and common laymen (be they autodidacts in matters of religion or not, alumni or not) who boldly began thereafter to "profess" preach and teach the Gospel their own-self-right-ways, (to maintain their opinions in matters of religion) and "interpret the Scriptures for themselves and others." All that also, because of excess of their confidence and conceit; and, "of futility in their thoughts."[18] Nay of relying particularly on their so-called common sense. And thus did sprout into a mushroom like hundreds of denominations and congregations with various and most often vicious and perilous doctrines, so that we can permit ourselves to proclaim vehemently with the Apostle Paul, "The name

---

[17]- *Harper and row, Publishers, Copyright 1964, pp. 207-208.*

[18]-*(Romans 1:22)*

of God is blasphemed among the Gentiles because of you, as it is written."[19]

Amazed and angry, the Apostle Paul writes to the Romans saying, "And how they preach unless they are sent?"[20]

Wondering and warning, he says to the Galatians, "But even if we, or an angel from heaven, preach any other gospel to you than what we have preached to you, let him be accursed."[21]

In the beginning of almost all his Epistles, Paul does bear witness to himself personally that he is sent by Christ himself to preach his gospel:

Thus, writing to the Romans he says, "Paul, a servant of Jesus, called to be an apostle, separated to the gospel of God."

In his first letter to the Corinthians, he writes, "Paul, called to be an apostle of Jesus Christ through the will of God."

---

[19]-*(Romans 2:24)*

[20]-*(Romans 10:15)*

[21]-*(Galatians 1:8)*

And in his second letter to them he says, "Paul, an apostle of Jesus Christ by the will of God."

To the Galatians he declares, "Paul, an apostle (not from men, nor through man, but through Jesus Christ and God the Father who raised him from the dead."

And to the Ephesians he announces, "Paul, an apostle of Jesus Christ by the will of God."

In his first letter to Timothy, Paul writes, "Paul, an apostle of Jesus Christ, by the Commandment of God our Saviour and the Lord Jesus Christ, our hope." And in his second letter to him, he says, "Paul, an apostle of Jesus Christ by the Will of God, according to promise of life which is in Christ Jesus."

And to Titus Paul writes saying, "Paul, a servant of God and apostle of Jesus Christ, according to the faith of God's elect and the acknowledgement of the truth which is according to godliness."

No, common sense is neither common philosophy, nor therapeutic theology, nor scientific reasoning, nor sociological sense of normal and common individuals.

And because individuals do differ most often drastically one from another in education and character, and sometimes in nature and degree, their common senses do differ accordingly. For what might be to one a matter of simple common sense, it might be total nonsense to another. And thus common sense, in general, is not always the only correct criterion, particularly in matters of religion.

Hence, here; the only true and genuine criterion or touchstone by which we can, somehow seize the real senses, mysteries and secrets of the Scriptures, comprehend and interpret them correctly, and somehow uniformly, is to refer, besides the Scriptures themselves, to the commentaries of the first and foremost fathers of the Church, universally known in their integrity, piety and sanctity.

However, the most surprising thing in America, is that every preacher, priest, pastor, and evangelist in the Protestant Church in general, affirms and confirms that he got directly from God, or Christ, or the Holy Spirit, or Heaven, or an angel, or the sacred Scriptures themselves, a special and particular call, or command, or exhortation, or revelation, or inspiration, or illumination, or voice, or the like to preach and teach the Gospel. (I do admit sincerely that some of them are very honest and trustworthy in their claim and vocation).

Consequently, every preacher and teacher of the Gospel in America, has his singular Church to head, his special congregation to run, his specific denomination to guide, his own flock to shepherd, his peculiar doctrine to defend, his particular priesthood to protect, his exclusive magazine to publish, his ceaseless series of books and cassettes to promote, and his proper program on radio and television to broadcast.

So no wonder again that "Denominational fission in Protestantism has produced in the United States (alone) over two hundred and fifty sects, and presents the movement launched by the Reformation with one of its most importunate problems."[22]

And Fosdick continues saying, "The ecumenical reaction has now set strongly in, and the Protestant churches, having moved out long since from mutual persecution to toleration, and from toleration to co-operation, now are headed from co-operation toward

---

[22]-*Great Voices of Reformation, by Harry Emerson Fosdick. The Modern Library, New York. Random House, Inc. Copyright 1952. P.545.*

unity. As a matter of fact about ninety percent of all Protestant church members in the United States are included within <u>twenty denominations</u>, so that the inefficiency and scandal of trivial division are not incurable, and intelligent leadership in all the churches is stressing ecumenical communion and unity as against partition."[23]

But unfortunately, the above mentioned "Twenty denominations" around the year 1952, (the very date of the publication of Fosdick's book) became nowadays hundreds of denominations in the United States alone as attests John Ross Schroeder: "There are hundreds of denominations on the American scene. Some big, some small-all differing in belief from other denominations to one degree or another. Everyone, it seems, is his own interpreter of the Bible."[24] As in his book Armageddon, Oil and the Middle East Crisis, says John F. Wallvorred, "The Protestant Church, in turn, multiplied into hundreds of denominations throughout the World."[25]

---

[23]-*Ibid Page 548.*

[24]- *Plain-Truth magazine May/June 1988. Man and Religion. PP 21,22.*

[25]-*Zondervan Publishing House. Grand Rapids, Michigan, Copyright 1990. P. 112.*

Now the important and most basic question is: Why again this fission, or partition, or split, of Protestantism, and especially in America is going on? Why do all these numerous and various denominations, congregations and churches exist "Some big, some small-all differing in belief from other denominations to one degree or another"? Why last but not least, does this continuous growing number of the so-called sectarian and heterodox movements that leads inevitably to the burgeoning and sprouting of "various and strange doctrines" using here Paul's statement in Hebrews 13:9?

From my perspective, the pure and simple response again is: Because of these so-called common sense, insights, or afflatus, or even whims and vagaries of individuals, each to interpret, translate, and transmit the Bible in his own way: "In the main, evangelicals did not simply become anti-intellectual, what they did was destroy the monopoly that classically educated and university trained clergymen had enjoyed. They threw theology open to any serious student of Scripture, and they considered the "common sense" intuition of people at large more reliable, even in the realm of theology, than the musing of an educated few."[26]

Thus, in so doing, again, the so-called "common sense" of people "at large" did monopolize in turn theology itself so that as Scriptures state, "Everyone did what was right in his own eyes."[27] Consequently, here again, everyone did form and reform his own reformation, and launched his bizarre belief, extravagant cult and creed, and so on and so forth.

And here, it is worth mentioning that even in the 19th Century this free will of individuals was behind divisiveness and diversities of churches in America as also reports George Marsden, "The democratic winnowing of the church produced not just pluralism but also striking diversity. . . Churches ranged from the most egalitarian to the most autocratic and included all degrees of organizational complexity. One could be a Presbyterian who favored or opposed the freedom of the will, a Methodist who promoted

---

[26]-*Evangelicalism And Modern America, Edited by George Marsden. William B. Eerdmans Publishing Company. Grand Rapids, Michigan, Copyright 1984. P.75.*

[27]-*(Judges 21:25)*

43

or denounced democracy in the church, a Baptist who advocated or condemned foreign missions, and a member of virtually any denomination who upheld or opposed slavery. One could revel in Christian history with John W. Nevin or wipe the slate clean with Alexander Campbell. The range of options within evangelical communions seemed virtually unlimited: One could choose to worship on Saturday, practice foot washing, ordain women, advocate pacifism, prohibit alcohol, or practice health reform. Or, like Abraham Lincoln, one could simply choose a biblical form of Christianity without the slightest ecclesiastical encumbrance."[28]

Yes indeed it is because of the free will of individuals and the freedom of speech according to the First Amendment, that the act of preaching and teaching the Gospel in America by vast and various number of individuals, [many clerical, corps, and corporations alike,] has become nowadays in a nut-shell:

I-A free forum for the distorting of the Scriptures and the sacrilege of the sacred alike.

---

[28]-Ibid. PP 76,77 ·

44

II-A fertile field for strange doctrines.

III-A highway for an easy Christianity.

IV-A blatant big business.

V-A real realm for psychiatry and pragmatism.

VI-A demonstrable display for performance and hilariousness.

It is about these five negative rather noxious aspects of preaching, I will endeavor to talk without any bias or slant or bigotry; and regardless of any belonging to any specific congregation or anticipative creed. And if I am exaggerating in the dealing of the matter and aggravating somehow, sometimes, the malady, it is for the sole purpose to shed the light (as many before me did) on its seriousness, and invite thereby parties and particular personalities to the dire task of treating it as a very urgent matter. And that is because of its direct effect on Christianity as a whole.

For, here too, America has become simultaneously a propitious and pernicious paradigm for all the people of the world through her prodigious power and prosperity, extreme liberty and excessive libertinism, apparent luring and luxurious life style (at least as exposed and exhibited in movies and videos spread all over the world). Alfred Balk put it this way, "Our political, cultural and economic weight has Americanized the world. . . Today the U.S. leads the world by far, because we have the largest economy and science-and-technology establishment; the new "World language" is English; the most contagious ideal is democracy; the benchmark currency is the dollar."[29]

According to the so-called teachings of sociology and history, it is always the younger that imitates the elder, and the weaker the stronger. Likewise, the conquered does emulate his conqueror in speech, customs, clothings, manners, moralities and immoralities as well. The Greek historian and essayist Plutarch (50?) said, "Greece the conquered, did conquer her conqueror i.e., the Romans." Through their victory over Greece, the Romans acquired willfully all Greek civilization and culture; so that almost in every Roman home there was a Greek tutor or educator.

"The Romans, as reports the World Book Encyclopedia, adopted Greek culture. Greek traditions lived on not only in Greece,

---

[29]-*The New York Times, Tuesday, July 31, 1990.*

but also in the writings of Roman orators and poets such as Cicero, Horace, and Virgil."[30]

Therefore a solemn day may come, no matter when in the early or distant future, in which all the people of the world may embrace deliberately and enthusiastically, if not specifically, the religion of the most civilized state or nation of the world, that is America, namely her virtues and vices as well as her ideals and idols simultaneously. But woe to that nation or state (endowed with God's only religion, the utmost perfect and divine religion) that defiles herself, and becomes in consequence "the stumble stone" and the perilous paragon to other nations and states. "For offenses must come, but woe to that person (or nation or state) by whom (or which) the offense comes."[31] Because those "who saw the wind (will) reap the whirlwind"[32] or "whatever a person sows, that he will also reap."[33]

---

[30]-*Copyright 1983, U.S.A. by World Book Incorporation.*

[31]- *(Matthew 18:7)*

[32]-*(Hosea 8:7)*

[33]- *(Galatians 6:7)*

47

This is not a pretentious or presumptuous prophecy. This is also the very scientific law of nature, history, and sociology. This is the law of things themselves indeed.

I

A FREE FORUM FOR THE DISTORTING OF THE SCRIPTURES AND THE SACRILEGE OF THE SACRED ALIKE

Will Durant says, "Luther defended the Bible as absolutely and literally true. He admitted that if the story of Jonah and the whale were not in the Scriptures, he would laugh at it as a fable; so too with the tales of Eden and the serpent, of Joshua and the sun; but, he argued, once we accept the divine authorship of the Bible we must take these stories along with the rest of as in every sense factual."[34]

However, it is Luther himself who somehow rejected systematically and simultaneously several books of the Bible as being not canonical in his own view. For instance:

From the Old Testament, he rejected categorically the Third Book of Esdras: "The Third Book of Esdras, he said, I throw into the Elbe." And about "the discourses of the

---

[34]-*The Story of Civilization. Simon and Schuster, New York; 1957 The Reformation (The Reformation in Germany) Page 371.*

Prophets", he also said, "were none of them regularly committed to writing at the time; then disciples and hearers collected them subsequently. . . Solomon's proverbs were not the work of Solomon."[35]

And from the New Testament, Luther also rejected three books: the two Epistles of both St. James and St. Jude, and the Apocalypse of St. John.

In his "Preface to the Epistles of St. James and St. Jude" he says about the first, "I do not hold it to be apostolic authorship, for the following reasons:

"Firstly, because, in direct opposition to St. Paul and all the rest of the Bible, it ascribes justification to works, and declares that Abraham was justified by his works when he offered up his son. St. Paul, on the contrary, in Romans 4:3, teaches that Abraham was justified without works, by his faith alone, the proof being in Genesis 15:6, which was before he sacrificed his son. . . This defect proves that the Epistle is not of apostolic provenance."[36]

---

[35]-*Ibid pp 370-371*

[36]-*Martin Luther. Selections from his Writings. Anchor Books Double day and Company, Inc. Edition 1961.*

But we have to notice here very carefully that God was revealed to Abraham the pagan, for the first time. As Abraham, for the first time also believed in Him. For when God promised that one "who will come from (his) own body shall be (his) heir"; and then brought him outside and showed him the innumerable stars, and said to him, "So shall your descendants be,"[37] at that very moment, Abraham "believed in the Lord, and he accounted it to him for righteousness."[38] Meaning here that Abraham's belief in the Lord as being the real and true God indeed, was certainly pure and perfect [even before he sacrificed his (future) son as says Paul.] However, when God, thereafter, promised Abraham also to give him the land of Canaan "to inherit it", we see the doubtful Abraham responding, "Lord God, how shall I know that I will inherit it?"[39] Abraham's faith was confirmed even though God recommended to him saying "Take now your only son Isaac, whom you love, and go to the land of Moriah,

---

Page 35.

[37]-*(Genesis 15:4,5)*

[38]- *(Genesis 15:1-6)*

[39]-*(Genesis 15:8)*

53

and offer him there as a burnt offering."[40] For Abraham obeyed God faithfully because he didn't refrain even from the slaying of his beloved and only son Isaac; although, by doing so, the promise of the Lord to him, "but one who will come from your own body shall be your heir"[41] would be obsolete and null; namely by the very death of Isaac. Therefore, here only, the satisfied God said to him "for <u>now</u> I know that you fear God,"[42] namely, "you believe truly in me and have firm faith in my promises."

Thus, it is to this very faith of Abraham in God accomplished by his willingness even to sacrifice his son to him, that James refers and reaffirms, "Do you see that faith was working together with his works, (i.e., when be offered his son Isaac to be slain on the altar) and by works faith was made perfect? And the Scripture was fulfilled which says, "Abraham believed God, and it was accounted to him for righteousness."[43] Meaning thus again, that the two apostles Paul and James are quite in full

---

[40]-*(Genesis 22:2)*

[41]-*(Genesis 15:4)*

[42]-*(Genesis 22:12)*

[43]- *(James 2:22,23)*

accord that faith in God or Christ is accomplished and made perfect by works. Therefore both faith and works are two necessary facts and factors for true righteousness and thereby for salvation "For as the body without the spirit is dead, so faith (alone) without works is dead too."[44]

Luther himself, the first and foremost advocator of "salvation through faith alone," declared emphatically in his Preface to the Romans, "It is impossible indeed, to separate works from faith; just as it is impossible to separate heat and light from fire."[45]

"Secondly, because, in the whole length of its teaching, not once does it give Christians any introduction or reminder of the passion, resurrection, or spirit of Christ. It mentions Christ once and again, but teaches nothing about him; it speaks only of a commonplace faith in God...(that is in fact the very first feeling of every meticulous reader of James' epistle). . . What does not teach Christ is not apostolic. . . I therefore refuse him a place

---

[44]-(James 2:26)

[45]-Ibid Page 24

among the writers of the true canon of my Bible. . ."[46]

It is proper to mention here that even Eusebius (third century) the most reliable historian of the Church, while writing about James' epistle, says, "Admittedly its authenticity is doubted, since few early writers refer to it, any more than to Jude's, which is also one of the seven called general. But the fact remains that these two, like the others, have been regularly used in very many churches."[47]

As for the latter, i.e., the Epistle of saint Jude, says Luther, "No one can deny that this epistle is an excerpt from, or copy of the second epistle of saint Peter, for all he says is nearly the same over again. . . He quotes words and events which are found nowhere in Scripture, and which moved the fathers to reject this epistle from the canon. . . Hence, although I value the book, yet it is not essential to reckon

---

[46]-Ibid Pp 35, 36

[47]-The History of the Church from Christ to Constantine. Translated by G.A. Williamson. Augsbury Publishing House. Minneapolis, Minnesoto, copyright 1965. Page 103.

it among the canonical books that lay foundation of faith."[48]

And also Luther does reject drastically the last book of the New Testament, namely the Book of Revelation or the Apocalypse. ". . . and at first, says Will Durant, he (Luther) rated the Apocalypse as an unintelligible farrago of promises and threats neither Apostolic nor Prophetic."[49]

Now, I do believe, that the statement of Luther's opponents, who ". . . predicted that after his example other critics would reject, according to their own tastes and views, other Scriptural books, until nothing would be left of the Bible as a basis for religious faith"[50] seems to be fulfilled, somehow verbatim, through the course of the American history. And that also in an unprecedented way by other thinkers, religious reformers, and various sects alike.

---

[48]-*Ibid. Pp. 36, 37*

[49]-*The Story of Civilization. The Reformation. Page* 370.

[50]-*Ibid. Page 371*

Although this prediction is applied on many examples, here are but few and in a bird's-eye view:

THOMAS JEFFERSON

As an eminent figure in the American History, and "The first political idealist among American statesmen and the real founder of the American democratic tradition,"[51] Thomas Jefferson, although reared in the Anglican Church, yet, as a layman, he expressed largely his unchristian faith that left undoubtedly its impact on the American life and belief as well.

For, his extreme belief in reason, per se, led him to lose his very faith in Religion in general, and in Christianity in particular.

Jefferson defines God in an Aristotelian way, namely through the utmost harmony in the universe and the dialectic of cause and effect. He says, ". . . it is impossible, I say, for the human mind not to believe that there is, in all this, design, cause and effect, up to an ultimate

---

[51]-*A History of the English-Speaking Peoples. By Winston S. Churchill. Dorset Press. Copyright 1957. New York (Volume 3. The Age of Revolution). Page 356.*

cause, a fabricator of all things from matter and motion,"[52] confirming whereby the pagan Greek dualism that says that God and matter to do exist abreast, and both are coeternal. Aristotle calls this "ultimate cause," Final Cause; Whereas in the Judeo-Christian dogma, there is no such dualism; God alone is the eternal one who created all things, included matter, out of nothing.[53]

Thomas Jefferson "firmly believed in God, but he could not accept the Christian concept of the Trinity. . . Jefferson's rejection of the Trinity is found throughout his writings . . . Jefferson's rejection of trinitarianism placed him in agreement with the deists and unitarians of his day."[54]

"Jefferson's reason compelled him to reject the Trinity; he could not accept Jesus Christ as the Son of God, the Second Person of the Godhead,"[55] even though, to him, Jesus was

---

[52]-*Christianity and the Constitution. By John Eidsmoe. A Mott Media Book. Baker Book House. Grand Rapids, Michigan. Copyright 1987. Page 223.*

[53]-*(Colossians 1:16)*

[54]-*Ibid. Pp. 224, 226*

[55]-*Ibid. P. 229*

"the most innocent, the most benevolent, the most eloquent and sublime character that ever has been exhibited to man."[56]

As Jefferson rejected the Bible itself. Says Eidsmoe here too, "Jefferson studied the Bible diligently; he read it in English, French, Latin, and Greek. But he did not regard it as the inspired Word of God. He could not accept any kind of revelation that contradicted or transcended reason, so he rejected the portions of the Bible which spoke of the miraculous and did not include them in his compilations of Bible verses: "The Philosophy of Jesus" and "The Life and Morals of Jesus."[57]

But I wonder, how this very man of reason, Thomas Jefferson, could believe, through reason, in the self-existence of an invisible God, (though material to him) then refuse and refute his existence at the same time, saying, "To talk of immaterial existences is to talk of nothings. To say that the human soul, angels, god (with small "g") are immaterial, is to say they are nothings, or that there is no god (always god here with small "g") no angels, no soul. I cannot reason otherwise:

---

[56]-*Ibid. P. 229*

[57]-*Ibid. P. 232*

but I believe I am supported in my creed of materialism by Locke, Tracy, and Stewart. At what age of the Christian Church this heresy of immaterialism, this masked atheism, crept in, I do not know. But a heresy it certainly is."[58] Again what a gibberish! What a gobbledygook!

Is it not because the impossibility of reaching God by reason (and believing in Him thereby) that Paul declared to the Corinthians, "For since, in the Wisdom of God, (i. e., the reason imparted by God to mankind or to the "world") the world through wisdom did not know God, it pleased God through the foolishness of the message preached to save those who believe?"[59] Meaning, that the true and very knowledge of God is through faith in Christ alone as being God alone. This very faith, Paul calls it "foolishness of the message."

Blaise Pascal (17th century) the French philosopher, mathematician, and, another great man of reason like Jefferson, defined "faith" that is "heart" or "in heart" in this wonderful way: "The heart has its reasons that reason

---

[58]-*Ibid. Pp. 235, 236*

[59]-*(1 Corinthians 1:21)*

doesn't know" (Le coeur a ses raisons que la raison ne connait point).[60]

Even Luther, another man of reason and logic too, said about reason, "All the articles of our Christian faith which God has revealed to us in His Word, are in presence of reason, sheerly impossible, absurd, and false. . . Reason is the greatest enemy that faith has. . . She is the Devil's greatest whore."[61]

About Jefferson's lack of faith, also says John Eidsmoe, "What Luther and others could not understand by human reason, they could affirm by faith in God's revelation; however Jefferson could not."[62]

---

[60]-Pascal. Oeuvres completes. editions du Seuil, 1963, Pensees. page 552.

[61]-The Story of civilization by Will Durant. The Reformation. Page 370.

[62]-Christianity and the Constitution. Page 221.

THE MORMONS

In "The Book of Mormon" Jesus Christ declares, "Behold, I am Jesus Christ the Son of God. I created the heavens and the earth, and all things that in them are. I was with the Father from the beginning, and the Father in me," and "I am the light and the life of the world. I am Alpha and Omega, the beginning and the end"[63] and, "Verily I say unto you, that the Father, and the Son, and the Holy Ghost are one; and I am in the Father, and the Father in me, and the Father and I are one."[64]

But in his Doctrine of Salvation, Joseph F. Smith, the founder of the Church of Jesus Christ and Latter-day Saints negates

---

[63]-*(3 Nephi 9:18)*

[64]*(3 Nephi 11:27)*
The Book of Mormon. Published by the Church of Jesus Christ of Latter-day Saints. Salt Lake City, U.S.A. 1986.

categorically the oneness of the Trinity. The seeming oneness of God is not in "essence." To him there is no one God, but rather several gods. "Jesus is greater than the Holy Spirit who is subject unto him." says also Smith. But "his father is greater than he is."[65]

Yet his most bizarre belief is:

That God "was once a man like us. . . dwelt on our earth, the same as Jesus Christ himself did."

That "step by step in the scale of progression, in the school of advancement; has moved forward and overcome until he has arrived at the point where he is now."

And that by the same process or progression "all men, are capable of being gods; and that god's angels and men are all of one species. . ."[66]

All this reminds us somehow of the Buddhism Nirvana, also a process or progression in which the individual, by the

---

[65]-Edgar P. Kaiser, How to respond to the latter-day saints, concordia publishing house, St. Louis. p. 14.

[66]-Ibid.

extinction of desire and successive reincarnations, is united with the supreme spirit.

The World Book Encyclopedia does report in turn that the Mormons "regard Jesus Christ as the first spirit-child, the Supreme Being <u>created</u>. They believe that Christ created the world under the direction of God the father."[67]

Among their other non Christian beliefs, "They further teach that the Father and Son have tangible bodies of flesh and bones" (Whereas the Apostle John does state, "God is Spirit, and those who worship him must worship in spirit and truth,"[68] and "God the Father is the literal parent or father of the spirits of all mortals. . . and Jesus was the first born in the spirit world . . ." and "Satan, who was another spirit Child of God. . ." and "The Holy Ghost or Holy Spirit, is a personage of spirit, meaning an entity or individual who is a spirit." As they "assert that God created the world by organizing chaotic matter. The word <u>create</u>,

---

[67]-*World Book Inc. A Scott Fetzer Company. Copyright 1983. U.S.A.*

[68]-*(John 4:24)*

they claim, means to organize, rather than to make out of nothing."[69]

Even though they accept the Bible as being the inspired Word of God "as far as it is translated correctly" as also reports the Encyclopedia Britannica, they do not, however, regard it as the sole and complete Word of God. Hence, they do add to it their own three other books: The Book of Mormon, Doctrines and Covenants, and the Pearl of Great Price.

---

[69]-*Christian Churches of America. By Milton V. Backman, Jr. Charles Scribner's Sons. New York. Copyright 1983. Page 178.*

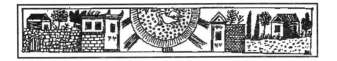

WATCH TOWER BIBLE
AND TRACT SOCIETY

Known also as Jehovah's Witnesses; they accept the Bible as being the inspired Word of God, and therefore inerrant. They, however, distort it drastically, to support, but to no avail, their false and bizarre beliefs. For instance, instead of accepting the authentic and genuine statement of John chapter one, verse one (as it is in the whole and diverse versions of the Bible since the beginning of Christianity) that states clearly, "In the beginning was the Word, and the Word was with God, <u>and</u> <u>the</u> <u>Word</u> <u>was</u> <u>God</u>" they translate it this way: ". . . and the Word was <u>a</u> <u>god</u> (god here with small "g") in purpose to make the Word or God who "became flesh"[70] that is Jesus Christ, inferior to God, or rather created by God. "God was once alone in the universe, they say, but after initiating the creation, Jehovah brought forth a son who was called "Michael" or the "Logos" (the "Word") in his premortal existence and

---

[70]-*(John 1:14)*

69

Jesus during his journey on earth. . . Jesus was not a god while residing on earth."[71]

Strangely enough, although they ascribe to Jehovah or God or Elohim, the whole creation in six days, as it is quite clear in chapter one of Genesis, yet they miss primarily John's chapter one and verse three, that ascribes (as in Genesis chapter one) the whole creation to Jesus Christ himself, or the Word or God or Elohim, that states, "All things were made through Him, and without Him nothing was made that was made." Meaning here and there, i.e., in Genesis and in John's gospel, that Jehovah or Elohim and Christ Jesus are one, and the only one God who created all things out of nothing.

Milton V. Backman, Jr. says: "While describing their belief concerning the Godhead, Jehovah's Witnesses explain that the Father and Son are separate and distinct spirits and the Holy Ghost is not a member of the Godhead, but is a divine influence or active force."[72] "Jehovah's Witnesses also teach that at the end of Christ's thousand-year reign on earth, all of God's children, except those beyond reform,

---

[71]-*Ibid. P. 201*

[72]-*Ibid. P. 201*

will gather for one last test (by Satan) and whoever remains loyal to God during this last trial (or test) will be blessed with eternal life."[73]

Their number is constant, they pretend, namely 144,000 according to Revelation 7:41.

---

[73]-*Ibid. P. 201*

HERBERT W. ARMSTRONG

Chairman of the World Wide Church of God for more than a half century; "In a time of cynical repudiation of moral values, Armstrong has vigorously affirmed the old-fashioned Christian and American virtues of honor, reverence, patriotism, thrift, integrity, chastity, and temperance."[74] But to Armstrong, unlike the overwhelming majority of Christians in the world, Saturday is the Sabbath that should be observed instead of Sunday.

Contrary to the teachings of the Bible from cover to cover, and like Thomas Jefferson, Armstrong rejects the doctrine of the Holy Trinity. Says James Morris "Time Magazine reported that the doctrines of Armstrongism included observance of Kosher laws set forth in the Old Testament, the Celebration of Passover

---

[74]-*The Preachers. By James Morris, St. Martin's Press. New York. Copyright 1973 (The Armstrongs. P. 320)*

but not of Christmas or Easter, and the denial of the Trinity."[75]

Armstrong's denial of the Trinity appears very clearly, for instance, in his booklet or brochure entitled "Never Before understood: Why Humanity cannot solve its evils" where he does not mention at all the Holy Spirit as being the third hypostasis (or Person) in the Holy Trinity. In page 4 of the above mentioned booklet or brochure, says Armstrong, "The Hebrew word translated "God" is Elohim, a uniplural noun like family, church or group. One family consisting of more than one person. God-Elohim- consisted from eternity of the "Word" and God-(not even God the Father but simply God)-Two Spirit- composed personages, forming one God, since the Word also was God. "As to him, like Jehovah's Witnesses, the Holy Spirit is not God but a force or influence or a gift of God. Namely again it is an "it" and not "the third hypostasy or person of the Holy Trinity."

Explaining John's statement "The Word was made flesh and dwelt among us,"[76]

---

[75]-*Ibid. Page 363*

[76]-*(John 1:14)*

Armstrong says "In other words, fathered by God, became by human birth, Jesus Christ."

Thus, to Armstrong, Godhead or Godhood or Elohim, is consisted from eternity of <u>two</u> <u>Gods</u>: of the Word (who was also God) and God. Two spirit-composed personages, forming one God (Pp. 3,4 of his booklet or brochure). Whereas in the Bible, from cover to cover, as in World Wide Christian belief since the beginning of Christianity heretofore, God, or Jehova, or the Word, or Elohim, in Hebrew Syriac Aramaic plural form "might be viewed...in the Christian view, as speaking in the persons of the Trinity."[77]

---

[77]-*Guide to the Bible. By Isaac Asimov. Avenue Books. New York. Avenel, 1981 Edition. P. 18*

ROBERT H. SCHULLER

In his book "Self-Esteem: The New Reformation" says Robert H. Schuller (who broadcasts his syndicated weekly Hour of Power from his Crystal Cathedral in Garden Grove, California,) "Somehow in our sincere effort to reform our church theology today, we must avoid the destructive and divisive results that occurred within the Church in the sixteenth century. Where the Protestant Reformation was a reactionary movement, the twentieth century Reformation must be a reconciling movement. Luther and Calvin, we know, looked to the Book of Romans in the Bible for their primary inspiration. Were they, unknowingly, possessed more by the spirit of St. Paul than by the Spirit of Jesus Christ? Are we not on safer grounds if we look to our Lord's words to launch our reformation?"[78]

---

[78]-*A Jove Book. Jove Edition/November 1985. Pp. 38,39.*

As we notice clearly in this paragraph, that I picked up at random, as a simple sampling of Schuller's teachings in his "New Reformation", he is "knowingly" offending:

First, the Protestant Reformation of having in fact "destructive and divisive results. . . within the Church in the sixteenth century."

Second, both Luther and Calvin, because of their looking "To the Book of Romans in the Bible for their primary inspiration" were therefore "unknowingly possessed more by the spirit (spirit here with small "s") of St. Paul than by the Spirit (Spirit here with capital "S") of Christ." Consequently, both Luther and Calvin, were not "on safe grounds" by doing so, i.e., by referring to St. Paul's letter to the Romans when they, for the first time, launched their Protestant Reformation.

Third, the spirit per se of Paul, of being neither adequate, nor genuine source of inspiration (in his Book of Romans) therefore, the dire necessity does require, so to speak, to the rejection of his "spirit" and thereby, to the rejection of his Book of Romans, and the recourse to Christ's words instead, for the "launching of Schuller's New Reformation."

But let us digress here a bit and report for a few instances what some noted Protestant theologians did say about the Book of Romans that Dr. Schuller seems, very knowingly, to neglect or disrespect.

In his Preface to the Romans says Martin Luther, father of Protestantism, "This epistle is in truth the most important document in the New Testament, the gospel in its purest expression. Not only is it well worth a Christian's while to know it word for word by heart, but also to meditate on it day by day. It is the soul's bread, or can never be read too often, or studied too much. The more you probe into it the more precious it becomes, and the better its flavor. . . Hitherto, this epistle has been smothered with comments and all sorts of irrelevances, yet, in essence, it is a brilliant light, almost enough to illuminate the whole Bible."[79]

And Dr. William Barklay, in, "The Daily Study Bible Series: the Letter to the Romans", says, "Romans, of all Paul's letters, comes nearest to being a theological treatise. In almost all his other letters he is dealing with

_____

[79]-*Selections from His Writings. Anchor Books. Doubleday and Company, Inc. Garden City, New York. Edition 1961. Page 19*

some immediate trouble, some pressing situation, some current error, some threatening danger, which was menacing the church to which he was writing. Romans is the nearest approach to a systematic exposition of Paul's own theological position, independent of any immediate of circumstances."

Because of that, two great scholars have applied two very illuminating adjectives to Romans. Sanday called Romans "testamentary." It is as if Paul was writing his theological last will and testament, as if to the Romans he was distilling the very essence of his faith and belief." Burton called Romans "prophylactic." A prophylactic is something which guards against infection. Paul had seen often what harm and trouble could be caused by wrong ideas, twisted notions, misguided conceptions of Christian faith and belief. He therefore wished to send to the Church in the city which was the center of the world a letter which would so build up the structure of their faith that, if infections should ever come to them, they might have in the true word of Christian doctrine a powerful and effective defense. He felt that the best protection against the infection of false teaching was the antiseptic of the truth."[80]

Now, as for the Spirit of Christ, it goes without saying, that it is other than the spirit of Paul. For Christ is God himself; whereas Paul is a common man indeed.

But as a sacred source of divine inspiration that delivered all his epistles, the Spirit[81] of Paul, is the self-same and very same Spirit of Christ or God himself. As attests Paul himself saying, "And I think I also have the Spirit[82] of God."[83]

And to the Thessalonians, writes Paul, that God has also given him "His Holy Spirit."[84]

As his love for the Corinthians is like that of God Himself when he states, "For I am jealous for you with godly jealousy. For I have betrothed you to one husband, that I may

---

[80]-*The Westminster Press. Philadelphia. Copyright 1975. The Introduction to the Letter to the Romans. P.p. 1,2.*

[81]-*(Spirit here with capital "S")*

[82]- *(Spirit here with capital "S")*

[83]-*(1 Corinthians 7:40 KJV)*

[84]- *(Thess. 1:8 KJV)*

present you as a chaste virgin to Christ."[85] For Christ did teach us saying, "a new commandment I give to you that you love one another as I have loved you."[86]

Isn't therefore, that whoever rejects Paul's Spirit, by whose inspiration delivered Christ's Gospel,[87] is rejecting thereby Christ's "words" as well?

Moreover, the Apostle Paul himself, in his letter to the Galatians, does address stern and severe warning against all who pervert the gospel of Christ: "But there are some who trouble you and want to pervert the gospel of Christ. But even we, or an angel from heaven, preach any other gospel to you than what we have preached to you, let him be accursed. As we have said before, so now I say again, if anyone preaches any other gospel to you than what you have received, let him be accursed."[88]

All this, to reiterate and reemphasize that there is no difference at all between

---

[85]-(2 Corinthians 11:2)

[86]-(John 13:34)

[87]- (in all his epistles)

[88]- (Galatians 1:7-9 KJV)

Christ's Spirit and Paul's spirit in the realm of inspiration of the Word of God in his Holy Bible. For what Paul says in his epistles is exactly, and textually, what Christ himself inspired him to write, no more, no less.

For again, and according to Paul's testimonies about himself:

He was called by Christ himself "A chosen vessel of mine."[89]

God himself "separated (him) even from (his) mother's womb and called (him) through his grace."[90]

The Gospel which he received and preached was not "according to man" neither "from man," nor was he "taught it, but it came through the revelation of Jesus Christ."[91]

The Thessalonians welcomed the word of God "which (they) heard from (him), (they) welcomed it not as the word of men, but as it is

---

[89]-(Acts 9:15 KJV)

[90]-(Galatians 1:15 KJV)

[91]-(Galatians 1:11,12 KJV)

83

in truth, the word of God, which also effectively works in (them) who believe"[92] etc., etc.

My question here to Dr. Schuller is: How many preachers and teachers of the Gospel in America, rather in the whole world, can dare proclaim from the very beginning of Christianity heretofore, what Paul emphatically proclaims in his above mentioned sayings?

---

[92]-(1 Thessalonians 2:13 KJV)

BISHOP JOHN S. SPONG

The 59-years old priest and bishop, John S. Spong, head of the Episcopal Diocese of Newark and father of three grown girls, seems to be chief among all apostate clergymen, and one of the most phenomenal figures in the whole of Christianity. For in his book "Rescuing the Bible from Fundamentalism,"[93] as reports Time Magazinc, February 18, 1991, "Jesus Christ, as reported in some New Testament passages, is "narrow-minded and vindictive." The Gospel writers "twisted" the facts concerning Jesus' resurrection, which has never meant to be taken literally. The virgin birth of Christ is an unthinkable notion, and there is not much value in the doctrine of the Trinity, or in the belief that Jesus Christ was sent to save fallen humanity from sin. Saint Paul, the missionary of Christianity to the Gentiles, was a

---

[93]-*(published February 1, 1991, Harper San Francisco)*

85

repressed and "self-loathing" homosexual. As for the Old Testament, it contains a "vicious tribal code of ethics" attributed to a "sadistic" God. The idea that Yahweh bestowed the Promised Land upon the Israelites is "arrogance", and so on, and so forth.

Thus, John S. Spong, even as a priest and bishop, is rejecting categorically and ironically both the Old and the New Testament and profaning the sacred thing pretentiously. For, as also reports the New York Times on Saturday, February 2, 1991, "Bishop Spong said his conclusions about St. Paul come from serious Bible study and from time he spends in libraries at Yale and Harvard and at Oxford and Cambridge during his annual month long study sabbaticals. If he did not eke out this time for study, he said, he would be overwhelmed by the administrative tasks of running his diocese, which has 125 churches in northern New Jersey. He has been in the post for 15 years."

And my question here: Why then as a priest and a bishop, and an alleged apostle of Christ, is offending Christ, reviling his saints, and sapping the sacred Scriptures? Why is he still sticking to the seat of bishopric, if not to suck and steal as a fake clergyman, as Judas, the continuous funds of the 125 churches

Northern New Jersey which he unreservedly runs to date? For only "those who preach the Gospel (and not offend it) should live from the gospel."[94]

About false apostles says St. Paul, "For such are false apostles, deceitful workers, transforming themselves into apostles of Christ. And no wonder! For Satan himself transforms himself into an angel of light."[95]

As for Bishop John S. Spong, as an alleged apostle, he is indeed called also "light" even by Christ himself: "you are the light of the world."[96] But, alas, "if therefore the light that is in you is darkness, how great is that darkness!"[97]

Yes, "how great is that darkness that is Spong!" It is indeed greater, much greater than all that we can conceive of and imagine. For again, when the Apostle Paul declares, "And no wonder! For Satan himself transforms himself

---

[94]-(1 Corinthians 9:14)

[95]-(2 Corinthians 11:13, 14)

[96]-(Matthew 5:14)

[97]-(Matthew 6:23)

into an angel of light"[98] he certainly could not go beyond such despicable and derisory description: "an angel of light." For to label Bishop S. Spong, God forbid, even as a transformed Satan into an angel of light, is somewhat to trivialize both terms: "Angel" and "Satan." For even Satan believed in Christ as God and Son of God, as the Scriptures attest[99] whereas Bishop S. Spong rejects categorically the virgin birth of Christ, his resurrection from the dead, and the Holy Trinity.

P. S. In America, News Media's policy in general, is to broadcast telecast and publish only and deliberately the sensational and the sensual, the salacious and the sacrilegious thing, and not the sacred thing at all. Recently, I have written an article and distributed to some Newspapers to be published, in response to Spong's offense to Scriptures generally, and to Paul particularly. But all of them declined to publish it. . . Therefore, I found it convenient to insert it, with a final remark, at the end of this chapter, as another adequate testimony to the decline of morality in this Great Country America, which has become, in this new age, a

---

[98]-(2 Corinthians 11:14)

[99]-(Mark 5:7 and James 2:19)

free forum for the distorting of Scriptures, and the dishonoring of the sacred thing.

But, alas, this same well-informed and informing media, is ignorant of two simple, new and old facts:

First: By distorting the Truth, it is depriving itself of the blessings of life and the grace of God.

Second:
By disseminating immorality, it is inescapably depraving itself.

Thus, in both cases, the News Media will ultimately destroy itself as the Scriptures say:

"He made a pit and dug it out and has fallen into the ditch which he made."[100] and "whoever digs a pit (i.e. to others) will fall into it."[101]

---

[100]-*(Psalm 7:15)*

[101]-*(Proverbs 26:27) and (Ecclesiastes 10:8)*

THE JESUS SEMINAR

Although countless of counterfeit versions of the Bible have been published through the course of history, yet the Sacred Word of God is still intact, untouchable, and unshakable like an everlasting sun in the firmament.

While thousands and thousands of years couldn't neither separate the Bible and Tradition as Tertulian (160, 220) the Carthegian theologian apologist and champion of Christology and trinitarianism says: "For only where the true Christian teaching and faith are evident will the true scriptures, the true interpretations, and all the true Christian traditions be found,"[102] nor "prevail against the

---

[102]-*Bible, Church, Tradition: An Eastern Orthodox View*, by George Florofsky, Translated into Arabic by father Michel Najim, page 97.

Church"[103] nor alter or obliterate one single iota in the Bible.

For again: Church and Bible do not separate. They are both united from the very beginning, as also attests Origen (185-254).[104]

However, nowadays, an insignificant group of so-called scholars, under the pretentious pseudonym of Jesus Seminar, is trying but to no avail, to eliminate "80% of words attributed to Jesus" as reports Los Angeles Times, Monday, March 4, 1991, saying, "The provocative Jesus Seminar on Sunday concluded six years of voting on what the Jesus of history most likely said, ruling out about 80% of words attributed to him in the Gospels and emerging with the picture of a prophet-rage who told parables and made pithy comments. "Virtually all of Jesus' words in the Gospel of John were voted down by scholars meeting in Sonoma (California), including a pulpit favorite verse, 3:16, "For God so loved the world that he gave his only Son."

---

[103]-*(Matthew 16:18)*

[104]-*Ibid p.114.*

The Jesus Seminar!   Again what an ironic nickname!   What a presumptuous nothingness!

When Christians were still an unknown minority, Jesus said to Saul while on his road to Damascus to persecute the few Christians there, "It is hard for you to kick against the goads."[105] And now, that the Gospel is, as has always been, the best seller in the entire world; and while Christians are populating and dominating the entire world, how much more impossible would it be for the poor and petty Jesus Seminar and the like to "Kick against the goads?"

P.S. It's while writing this chapter, that I received from my daughter (in Los Angeles) the Los Angeles Time, Monday, March 9, 1991 copy that reported "this" funny or flimsy endeavor of the so-called Jesus Seminar. A mere coincidence you may say, but no; for the endless sacrilege of the sacred will continue, but to no avail, as used to be the case, since the beginning of Christendom.

Therefore, on the basis of the following Turkish proverb related by Dostoievski in "The Diary of a Writer:"

---

[105]-(Acts 9:1-5)

"If thou hast started out to reach a certain goal, and if thou shouldst be stopping en route to throw stones at every dog barking at thee, thou shalt never reach thy goal."[106] I would like to end this futile argument with "the Jesus Seminar," lest I miss really my ultimate goal. But here, it is again this single and simple word "dog" (in this Turkish proverb) that reminds me, by the spontaneous, marvelous and sometimes malicious "association of ideas," of a certain saying by a stupendous saint, not less, to me, than the Apostle Paul, in his very devotion to Christ, and assault against heresies. His name is St. Ephraim the Syrian (4th Century). Comparing himself to a sheepdog guarding the sheep of Christ, St. Ephraim says in his death-bed noted Testament:

> "I never ever scolded a person,
> Nor I quarreled with anybody since I existed.
> But with the Apostates, every moment
> I used to yell in the assemblies.
> For, you know, when the dog watches
> the wolf attacking the flock,
> if he doesn't rush to bark at him,
> his master will come and batter him"
> Oh what a man here! And what men there!

---

[106]-*Translated and annotated by Boris Brasol. New York, George Braziller 1954, Copyright 1949. Page 197.*

HOW DID PAUL DEAL WITH THE TOPICS:
SIN, WOMEN AND MARRIAGE

(A terse treatment, in response again to Bishop
John S. Spong)

In his life, few epistles, and up till his
martyrdom, Paul, a rabid rabbi (before and
after his conversion) is undoubtedly considered
as the first and foremost champion in shaping
Christianity. Jesus Christ called him "a chosen
vessel of mine."[104] As he (Paul) urged the
Corinthians to imitate him, as he also imitated
Christ.[105] Even before his conversion, Paul was,

---

[104]-*(Acts 9:15)*

[105]-*(1 Corinthians 11:1)*

95

"concerning the righteousness which is in the law, blameless" as he wrote to the Philippians.[106]

Talking about Paul's letters, Tolstoy puts it this way, "How strange and odd it would have seemed to educated Romans of the middle of the first century that the letters addressed by a wandering Jew to his friends and pupils would have a hundred, a thousand, a hundred thousand times more readers and more circulation than all the poems, odes and elegies and elegant epistles of the authors of those days (and of these also) and yet this is what has happened."[107]

No one loved Christ as Paul did. For to him (to Paul), to live was Christ, and to die was gain.[108] However, his love to his people, the Israelites, was somehow even more amazing. He loved them more than any Christian or Jewish human being. He loved them not only to the degree of self-denial, but rather of self-damnation; and even the denial of Christ himself, for whom he was decapitated by Nero's

---

[106]-(Philippians 3:6)

[107]-Paul the Leader, by Oswald Sanders-Naupress. Second printing 1964, page 58.

[108]-(Philippians 1:21)

sword. For he wished earnestly, that "he himself were accursed from Christ for his brethren, his kinsmen, the Israelites, to whom pertain the adoption, the glory, the covenants, the giving of the law, the service of God and the promises of whom are the fathers and from whom, according to the flesh, Christ came, who is over all, the eternally blessed God", as he wrote to the Romans.[109]

Even his opponents, are to this day adulating his righteousness and heroic faith. Says, for instance, Solomon Grayzel in his "History of the Jews," 'He (Paul) has spoken in terms of high and noble idealism, of charity, of personal righteousness. He urged men to believe in Jesus firmly and, believing in so perfect an example of godly living, begin to lead a godly life themselves.[110]

And Dr. Pinhas Lapide, the Orthodox Jewish and German theologian, says about Paul, "But through his lifetime, his people remained Israel. His Bible was the Tanak, his God was the God of his fathers, his Messiah was a Jew, and from Jews alone emerged his mother

---

[109]-(Rom. 9:3-5)

[110]-Philadelphia. The Jewish Publication Society of America. Copyright 1947, page 152.

church. . . He was a son of Israel, a religious fanatic and missionary before the Damascus experience and afterward; and remained so until his death on a Roman cross. . . but above all else he is a hero of the faith-not of lukewarm rational pistis of the philosophers, but of the incandescent Hebraic emuna; a person who in his initial experience of faith perceived the vocational calling to which he dedicated his entire life."[111]

SIN

In the Jewish-Christian view, sin is under every ceiling, dwelling every human being. "There is none righteous, no, not one" as says David.[112] And, when Paul is calling himself "a wretched man" and even "a chief" of sinners as he writes to Timothy[113] it is because of sin "dwelling in him" or "in his flesh" or "in his members"[114] and every human member. For as he again wrote to the Romans, "just as through

---

[111]-*Paul Rabbi and Apostle. Translated by Lawrence W. Denef-Augsburg Publishing House, Minneapolis, Copyright 1984, p.p. 43,47,54.*

[112]-*(Psalm 14:1. and Romans 3:10)*

[113]-*(I Timothy 1:15)*

[114]-*(Romans 7:17,18,23)*

one man sin entered the world and death through sin, and thus death spread to all men because all sinned."[115]

Thus, Paul is reverberating and repeating:

What Moses himself declared in Genesis (6:5) that the Lord "himself saw the wickedness of man was great in the earth, and that every intent of the thoughts of his heart was only evil continually."
And what job pleaded, "Can mortal man be righteous before God? Can a man be pure before his Maker?"[116]

And what David agonized over 'Behold, I was brought forth in iniquity and in sin my mother conceived me."[117]

And what Isaiah proclaimed "But we are all like an unclean thing, and all our righteousness are like filthy rags" (64:6) etc. etc...

---

[115]-(Romans 5:12)

[116]-(Job 4:17)

[117]-(Psalm 51:5)

But the most saddening and stunning, is that most of the clergymen in general, and religious leaders in particular, the so called "light of the world," seem to be (always) the last ones in all generations past and present, to read the word of God in his sacred Scriptures;" as it was in the time of Jesus, and as attest here too the Scriptures themselves: "you, search the Scriptures, for in them you think you have eternal life; and these are they which testify of men"[118] and "have you not read what David etc..."[119] and "have you never read what David etc. . ."[120] and "have you not read this Scriptures etc. . .[121] and " have you not even read this etc. . .[122] They are rather, sad to say, (especially nowadays in America): fortune-tellers, book-sellers, advice-donors, joke-crackers, riddle-solvers, Scripture-slanders,

---

[118]-*(John 5:39)*

[119]-*(Matthew 12:3)*

[120]-*(Mark 2:25)*

[121]-*(Mark 12:10)*

[122]-*(Luke 6:3)*

slander-utterers and "prayer-bombardiers,[123] and so on.

It is very strange indeed that a renowned, reckless, pretentious clergyman, a married bishop, and a father of three grown daughters, named John S. Spong, outrageously accused Paul of homosexuality.[124] Contrary to this, Paul vehemently warned the Corinthians that "homosexuals will not inherit the kingdom of God."[125] No, no wonder, for even God himself is reviled and denied almost every day by secular philosophers and fools: (the fool has said in his heart, "There is no God."[126]

WOMAN

Moreover, it is very sad, strange and shocking that this same presumptuous minister John S. Spong, accuses Paul, the greatest saint

---

[123]-*Norman Vincent Peale. The power of Positive Thinking, Copyright 1987 by Prentice Hall Press, New York, p.p. 52,53.*

[124]-*The New York Times Metropolitan Section, Saturday, Feb. 2,1991.*

[125]-*(1 Corinthians 6:9)*

[126]-*(Psalm 53:1)*

of Christendom, for his apparent hostility towards women and the fact that he never married.

For Paul, was also, rather the first and foremost champion of women's rights. Even in both the Old and the New Testaments, as in all other religions, no one granted women their noble and stupendous status save Paul. Moreover, his general attitude towards women' almost in all of his letters, is marked by great honor, courtesy, and consideration as his statements show in the following:

Equating women with men, and all in Christ, he wrote to the Galatians saying emphatically: "There is neither Jew nor Greek, there is no slave nor free, there is neither male nor female; for you are all one in Christ Jesus."[127]

To the Corinthians he declared that man "is the image and glory of God; but woman is the glory of man"[128] making thereby woman God's glory's glory indeed!

---

[127]-(Galatians 3:28)

[128]-(1 Corinthians 11:7)

After confirming Genesis 2, says Paul "for man is not from woman 'but woman from man, nor was man created for the woman, but woman for the man,"[129] then he adds "Nevertheless, neither is man independent of woman, nor woman independent of man, in the Lord. For as the woman was from the man, even so the man also is through the woman; "but all things are from God."[130]

To eliminate and abolish all sorts of unfair treatment of women throughout the dark and barbarous ages, Paul in Ephesians, urges wives to "submit to <their> own husbands, (meaning to be faithful and trustworthy to them) as to the Lord. For the husband is head of the wife, as also Christ is head of the Church" (5:22,23) (meaning here also, in a spiritual, hierarchical way and not at all in an authoritative or autocratic manner). For he adds, putting always the stress and emphasis on "love, pure love of Christ himself" who died also for the sake of mankind, or the church: "Husbands, love your wives, just as Christ also loved the church and gave himself for it... So husbands ought to love their own wives (meaning to abstain from fornication) as their

---

[129]-(I Corinthians 11:8,9)

[130]-(1 Corinthians 11:11,12)

103

own bodies; he who loves his wife loves himself."[131]

Thus, as long as the Book of History is written by man alone and not by woman and man simultaneously (i.e., one page written by man and another by woman); or inasmuch as Religions, Laws, Constitutions, and Institutions are made by man alone; and War and Peace are held in the firm fist of man only, man will always remain the head of woman, and woman will, willy-nilly, and unfortunately, submit to man" as is was the custom in the past days of paganism, but not at all in the Christian way of Paul, which is dramatically and diametrically opposed to.

In Paul's view and vision, the relationship of man and woman is sacred, spiritual, and sublime. Whereas that of the world is merely corporal, carnal, and pragmatic. In the first, "love" (between man and woman) is sanctified. In the latter "love is exploitation" as Sartre defines love; namely utilization and utilitarianism. In the first, marriage is powerful, permanent, and no one can put it asunder save death.[132] In the latter, marriage is feeble,

---

[131]-*(Ephesians 5:25,28)*

[132]-*(1 Corinthians 7:39)*

104

fragile, and apt to being nullified at any time, by any bylaw or the fallacious fiat of any worldly judge.

As for his prohibiting women from teaching and his commanding them to be silent in the churches[133] it is perhaps because women, in general, at that time, were not as educated as men. For we see him on the other hand giving special appreciation and even adulation to many of them like "Phoebe our sister, who is a servant of the church in Cenchrea." and "Mary," who labored much for us". . . "and Junia," as he writes to the Romans 16:1,7. And as Euodia and Syntyche "who labored with me in the gospel,"[134] and Prisca, wife of Aquila and Claudia.[135]

MARRIAGE

Nobody like Paul wrote so rightfully, so thoroughly, and so powerfully about the sanctity of marriage. This "great mystery," he calls it in Ephesians (5:32), another pretext and plea, that

---

[133]-*(1 Corinthians 14:34)*

[134]-*(Philippians 4:3)*

[135]-*(2 Timothy 4:19)*

the ungodly attack him and distort his teachings.

First and foremost Paul is against polygamy: "Because of sexual immorality let each man have his own wife, and each woman her own husband."[136]

And because self-control, discipline and subjection of the body are not given to all as they were his,[137] "it is better (then), he teaches, to marry than to burn with passion."[138]

Also to him, marriage is "honorable among all, and the bed undefiled; but fornicators and adulterers God will judge."[139]

And contrary to those who label him as being an anti-feminist and anti-marriage, we see him writing to Timothy to "instruct the brethren" to take heed of "some who, in latter times, will depart from the faith, giving heed to deceiving spirits and doctrines of demons,

---

[136]-(I Corinthians 7:2)

[137]-(1 Corinthians 9:27)

[138]-(1 Corinthians 7:9)

[139]-(Hebrews 13:4)

106

speaking lies in hypocrisy, forbidding to marry etc.."[140]

Last but not least, why Paul never married? And why did he wish that all men were even as he himself was?[141]

Simply speaking, it was to devote himself utterly to the preaching of Christ Jesus whom he loved even unto martyrdom. Does the 59 year old bishop John S. Spong ignore even this very fact? If so, he is again, in fact, the most miserable man!

---

[140]-(1 Timothy 4:1-3)

[141]-(1 Corinthians 7:7)

FINAL REMARK

Now, I would like to close this chapter with this final, funny, and frank remark that hurts only the feelings of those who fault expressly the Scriptures and hate the truth:

The first and foremost eye and ear witnesses of Jesus' wonderful words and wonders, were of course his disciples and apostles. They were also the very narrators and preachers of his teachings, miracles and signs. As, by the help of the Holy Spirit, they documented them fully, faithfully, and very accurately in the following canonical books from the very beginning of Christendom.'[142]

- The four Gospels of Matthew, Mark, Luke and John.
- The book of Acts.
- The 21 Epistles of the Apostles, Paul, James, Peter, John and Jude.
- The Book of Revelation. (Even though recognized and canonized lately)

---

[142]- *Eusebius: The History of the Church - Augsburg Publishing House, Minneapolis, Minnesota, Copyright 1965, p.p. 131-135.*

And, through the above mentioned Scriptures they did delineate Christ Jesus as being:
- The very Son of Man via David's lineage.
- The very Son of God before all ages.
- The very omnipotent, omniscient, and omnipresent God himself, who performed all his miracles, wonders and signs by his own will and proper power.

As they, namely his Disciples and Apostles, testified, till martyrdom:

- His crucifixion, death, resurrection, ascension to heaven; and his promise to come to earth in like manner as they have seen him ascend into heaven; but, to judge, this time, the living and the dead, each according to his good or bad works and deeds indeed.

Yet, the most amazing, ironic, and unusual alike, is that some insignificant minority, composed of some petty puppets, pseudo-prophets, and so-called scholars and philosophers, such as Renan, Jefferson, Tolstoy, Nietzsche and the like, albeit departing from the self-same Scriptures, principally the New Testament, as their sole and single reference, they, however, depicted a Jesus of their own: Namely deprived and debarred almost from all his prerogatives as being God, Son of God,

Creator, and performer of all the miracles he wrought and the teachings he taught, as it is related truly and textually in the Bible.

They did all that exactly as some Spongists and Napoleon Bonaparte seminar so to say, who would come, today, corroborate, confirm and reaffirm to us, always on basic and according to all the books written about Napoleon, that:

- He was only and solely a simple actor, poet and teacher, who also wrote some short stories.

- He never, ever mobilized any armies, waged any wars, conquered any country, or shed any blood whatsoever.

- He finally died at the age of 52 (the only correct fact) as a pauper, in a certain slum on the outskirts of Paris.

Now again, the crucial question here: why did all these so-called eminent thinkers distort and mutilate the Scriptures to depict a Jesus of their own?

Answer: For the pure and simple reason that they were practicing evil; and "everyone practicing evil hates the light and does not come to the light, lest his deeds should be exposed."[143]

And, because they want to live in a world without God, so that every evil deed would be permissible and palatable to them, such as lie, robbery, murder, rape, adultery, fornication, incest, illegal marriage and remarriage, divorce and the like.

Chataubriannd, the French author and statesman (1768-1848), nearly fifty years before Dostoyevsky, put it this way, "When men loose the idea of God, they presipitate into all crimes in spite of laws and executioners."[144]

Even Karamazove of Dostoyevsky will say, "If God does not exist, then, everything is permissible."[145]

Moreover, because Christ Jesus of the Scriptures, as the only judge,[146] does condemn such wicked people to everlasting death and torment in hell.

---

[143]-*(John 3:20)*

[144]-*Genie du Christianisme I-Garnier-Flammarion 1966, Paris, the introduction page 51.*

[145]-*Ibid.*

[146]-*(Psalm 50:6 and John 5:27)*

112

II

A FERTILE FIELD FOR STRANGE DOCTRINES

THE DOCTRINE OF "WRATH-OFFERING"

Among the strangest doctrines that some American pastors and Evangelists teach, and preach, and publish nowadays, competing and challenging somehow one another and sometimes even themselves, is the following:

That Christ, because of his bearing upon himself the sins of humanity, and being thereby our substitute and passover, did truly "suffer on his cross the very wrath of God" or "spent the equivalent of eternity in hell" (as heralds Harold Camping almost every day on his daily radio program, "Open Forum.")

That, "My God, My God why has thou forsaken me?" was Christ's encounter with hell. In that "hellish" death our Lord experienced the ultimate horror - humiliation, shame, and loss of pride as a human being. A person in hell when he has lost his self-esteem. Can you imagine any condition more tragic to leave life and eternity in shame?"[147]

That, "He (Christ) experienced hell on the cross. For He experienced the loss of glory and total humiliation and shame when he was crucified as a common criminal and hung naked? How they scorned him," He saved others - himself he cannot save! "He experienced total loss of self-esteem that turned hours of shameful exposure into an eternity in hell."[148]

That, "Christ descended into Hell, meaning that He endured the very wrath of judgement of God, and that upon the cross in body and soul, He endured not only the incredible agony of crucifixion which are beyond our explanation or comprehension, but more than that. In His soul, He experienced the very infinite wrath of God as the God Man, the Anthropos. He, in His own body endured the infinite wrath of God for a finite time. He had

---

[147]-*Self-Esteem: The New Reformation, by Robert H. Schuller. A Jove Book. Jove Edition/November 1985. The Introduction. pp.14,15.*

[148]-*Ibid. Page 101.*

often spoken of hell and the wrath of God. Upon the cross He experienced it."[149]

That, "Jesus did not merely die, or did He merely cast Himself into the teeth of the wolves, but He threw Himself into the very maw of the wrath of God. We may not tell, we cannot know, what pain He had to bear. Jesus descended into hell. He endured not merely physical death, but spiritual death - eternal death - the wrath of God poured out upon Him. Here the fire and the brimstone that consumed Sodom and Gomorrah fall upon Him as the sin bearer of the world, that innocent substitute who was now consumed by the molten lava of the wrath of God."[150]

"He (the Lord of heaven) pours out the caldron of His wrath upon His own Son. Jesus Christ, in His own body and soul, endures the infinite penalty for our sin."[151]

---

[149]-"*He descended into hell*", *a published sermon or brochure (without date) by D James Kennedy, Ph.D., Pastor of the Coral Ridge Presbyterian Church in Fort Lauderdale, Florida.*

[150]-*Continuing Communion. Another sermon by Dr. D. James Kennedy. P.4.*

[151]-*Justification by Faith. A sermon or brochure by Dr. D. James Kennedy. P.3.*

That, "To the Scriptures "Cup" is used figuratively to describe either God's blessing[152] or God's wrath.[153] Since Jesus would not have prayed for God's blessing to be taken from him, it is obvious that his use of "Cup" here speaks of the divine wrath that Christ would suffer at the cross as he bore the sins of mankind upon himself."[154] etc. etc. etc.

Now, what more horrendous and harmful statements were ever told about Christ than these?! Certainly Scriptures denounce them drastically, and even Protestantism as a whole disapproves them decisively. Even Common Christian Sense disdains and dismisses them outright!

It seems to me here, that despite their real zeal, integrity, and fervent faith in Christ, most of these sentimentalist teachers and preachers of the Gospel unfairly inferred such a daring doctrine. Influenced, maybe, by C. Spungeon, Lockyer and others, they have been deceived, and gone astray:

---

[152]-(Psalms 23:5)

[153]-(Psalms 75:8)

[154]-"Facing Death and the Life After "by Billy Graham. Decision, January 1988.

118

First: In his 20th sermon entitled "Justification By Grace" Rev. C. Spurgeon, the eloquent British preacher of the 19th Century (1834) says, "The whole of the punishment of his (Christ) people was distilled into one cup; no mortal lip might give it so much as a solitary sip. . . He drunk it all, he endured all, he suffered all; so that now forever there are no flames of hell for them, no racks of torment; they have no eternal woes; Christ hath suffered all they ought to have suffered, and they must, they shall go free. . . If God had not accepted his sacrifice, he would have been in his tomb at this moment, he never would have risen from his grave."[155] [As if Christ himself was not God himself, who by his own will and proper power "died and rose again."[156] For as he himself attested, ". . . I lay down my life that I may take it again. . . I have to lay it down, and I have power to take it again"[157]]

Secondly, the noted author of "All Series Of Bible Study and Reference Books" Dr. Lockyer, in spite of being considered so "uncompromisingly evangelical and possessed of

---

[155]-*Spurgeon's Sermons, Volume 3. Baker Book House. Grand Rapids, Michigan 49506; Reprinted 1985. Pp. 298, 299.*

[156]-*(1 Thessalonians 4:14)*

[157]-*(John 10:17,18)*

119

expository gifts of rare and engrossing quality" (See the covers of his Series), and despite his capability of compilations (of course through Bible concordances and indexes) and piling of publications in series, yet, many of his theological commentaries and endeavors in this realm, are most often erroneous, dreadful, and deceitful.

It is in his book "All the Doctrines of Bible" and under the title "The Doctrine of Substitution" that he coined his bizarre, and unbiblical expression "Wrath-Offering" saying, "Christ in his death became our propitiation, or wrath-offering. . . He bore the wrath due to our sins."[158]

And the references he gives to support the fallacy of his pretensions are the following:

-Romans 3:25 that states, "Whom God set forth to be a propitiation by his blood, through faith."

-Romans 5:9 that states, "We shall be saved from wrath through him."

-1 Corinthians 5:7 that states, "For indeed Christ our Passover was sacrificed for us."

---

[158]-*Zandervan Books, Grand Rapids, Michigan, copyright 1964. Page 185.*

Now, from the above-mentioned three statements of the Apostle Paul, we notice:

Firstly, from Romans 3:25, that Christ, "by his blood" (or sacrifice, or crucifixion) "became our propitiation through faith" (and not a wrath-offering) so that we are saved.

Secondly, from Romans 5:9, it is again by Christ or through Christ alone that we are saved from the wrath of God; and not at all, because he himself ("the lamb without blemish and without spot" as says 1 Peter 1:19) became, God forbid, a target for the wrath of God.

Thirdly, from 1 Corinthians 5:7, that Christ, our Passover was sacrificed for us - but by his own will and proper power[159] - and not at all, God forbid, by being he himself thereby a very sinner so that he should be punished accordingly by God, and suffer his very wrath.

Thus, the fact of humiliating himself by being flesh,[160] namely in the seeming flesh of sin, or "in the likeness of sinful flesh"[161] -For he was even baptized as a seeming common sinner also, in the purpose "to fulfill all

---

[159]-(John 10:18)

[160]-(John 1:14)

[161]-(Romans 8:3)

121

righteousness"[162] - but without losing, or ceding, or conceding his divinity, he did expose himself in order to take, as Paul says in Philippians 2:8,9, "the form of a servant" and to become "obedient to the point of death, even the death of the cross" (and not at all to suffer also the wrath of God). "Therefore God also has highly exulted him". (And not at all, God also "has shamed or disgraced or dishonored or punished him or poured out upon him his wrath") "and given him the name which is above every name." (And not at all, here too, and "deprived him of his self-esteem" or "consumed him by the molten lava of the wrath of God.") And to be made "little lower than the angels (while they were still and as always and forever worshipping and serving him,[163] for the suffering of death (and not of "wrath of God,") crowned with glory and honor (And not, God forbid, "with shame and humiliation"), that by the grace of God (and not by his fierce wrath) He might taste death for everyone"[164] and not again "taste the wrath of God from the "cup" he asked to be taken away from him.

Consequently, the fact itself of being also "hanged on a tree" did label him "a curse for

---

[162]-*(Matthew 3:15-15)*

[163]-*(John 1:51 and Luke 22:43)*

[164]-*(Hebrews 2:9)*

122

us"[165] or "sin for us"[166] or to be called also "a sinner" and "a friend of tax collectors and sinners."[167] But without becoming, he himself, "who knew no sin,"[168] "guilty of murder, of hate, of jealousy, of adultery, of everything."[169]

For, he who willingly paid all your debts, that does not mean that he personally was in fact indebted to all your own creditors.

As he who willfully accepted to pay the penalty for all your crimes and murders and even to die by crucifixion for all that, do not say, if you please, that he himself was in fact, or became accordingly guilty of all your monstrous malefactions and sinful sins.

No, very reverend "sirs" and "seers," Christ was guilty of nothing that he endured the cross. But on the contrary, even while agonizing at his cross, Christ did always please God his Father. As he pleased him particularly at that very moment i.e., at his cross. For:

---

[165]-*(Deuteronomy 21:23 and Galatians 3:13)*

[166]-*(2 Corinthians 5:21)*

[167]-*(Matthew 11:19 and Luke 7:34)*

[168]-*(2 Corinthians 5:21)*

[169]-*Decision, March 1988. "In the midst of pressures: The Choice is Yours", by Billy Graham.*

"From the sixth hour until the ninth hour there was darkness over all the land."[170]

"The sun was darkened."[171]

"The veil of the temple was torn in two from top to bottom."[172]

"The earth quaked, and rocks were split."[173]

"The graves were opened, and many bodies of the souls who had fallen asleep were raised, went into the holy City, and appeared to many."[174]

"The centurion. . . and those with him. . . feared greatly, saying "Truly this was the Son of God."[175]

Now, all these spectacular, stupendous, and supernatural signs took place while Christ

---

[170] -(Matthew 27:45 and Mark 15:33 and Luke 23:44)

[171] -(Luke 23:45)

[172] -(Matthew 27:51 and Mark 15:38 and Luke 23:45)

[173] -(Matthew 27:51)

[174] -(Matthew 27:52)

[175] -(Matthew 27:54 and Mark 15:39 and Luke 23:47)

was agonizing on his cross. Were they because of the falling of the wrath of God upon him, or rather upon "the rulers of the world" who crucified Christ "the Lord of glory", as they are still unknowingly doing so every day?

No, Christ endured suffering and death on the cross not in his soul at all, but rather in his body as the Apostle Peter reveals that in the following inspiring words saying, "Therefore, since Christ suffered for us <u>in the flesh,</u> arm yourselves also with the same mind, for he who has suffered <u>in the flesh,</u> has ceased from sin."[176] Consequently has ceased from the wrath of God also. For the wrath of God is poured out only and solely upon sinners. And sinners alone do die physically, mentally, morally, spiritually and eternally. Because "the wages of sin is death."[177] Again, Peter asserts: Christ "suffered once for sins, the just for the unjust, that he might bring us to God, being put to death <u>in the flesh</u> but made alive by the Spirit."[178]

---

[176]-*(1 Peter 4:1)*

[177]-*(Romans 6:23)*

[178]-*(1 Peter 3:18)*

125

If Christ, "the lamb of God" took away the sin of the world,[179] it is only in the sense that by his willful sacrifice, he accepted even to be crucified so that he nailed our sin to his cross[180] and not at all because by being our passover, or propitiation, he suffered the wrath of God.

Since "he was led as a lamb to the slaughter, and as a lamb before its shearers is silent, so he opened not his mouth."[181] Christ by doing so, became not at all "a wrath-offering" as says Dr. Herbert Lockyer, but rather "an Aromatic-Offering" or "a Spicy-Sacrifice" as the Apostle Paul asserts: "And walk in love, as Christ also has loved us and given Himself for us, an offering and a sacrifice to God for a sweet-<u>smelling</u> <u>aroma</u>."[182]

Thus again, Christ used to do always the things that pleased his Father.[183] As God his Father has been always and in all cases "well

---

[179]-*(John 1:29)*

[180]-*(Colossians 2:14)*

[181]-*(Isaiah 53:7)*

[182]-*(Ephesians 5:2)*

[183]-*(John 8:29)*

126

pleased" in him.[184] If so, how then can one imagine, or dare think of the unbiblical idea that God the Father punished him because he voluntarily bore the sin of humanity? Isn't God the Father himself who gave him that very cup as Jesus asserts to Peter saying, "Shall I not drink the cup which my Father has given me?"[185]

Let us consider his plea to the Father: "Let this cup pass from me", or "Take this cup from me,"[186] or "Remove this cup from me."[187] No, Christ did not mean at all by that "the cup of the divine wrath of God" but rather the very atrocious cup of death; crucifixion itself; or the "horrors of such a death." For Christ himself did make that abundantly clear when, addressing Zebedee's sons, he said, "You will indeed drink my cup."[188] Meaning again the cup of suffering till martyrdom.[189] For they also "will

---

[184]-(Matthew 3:17 and Mark 1:11 and Luke 3:21 and 2 Peter 1:17)

[185]-(John 18:11)

[186]-(Mark 14:36)

[187]-(Luke 22:43)

[188]-(Matthew 20:23 and Mark 10:39)

[189]-(Acts 12:1,2)

suffer for his sake,"[190] although John, James' brother, will be spared from Herod's sword.

Talking about Christ's suffering and supplications, it is the Apostle Paul here too, who discloses this mystery saying, "In the days of his flesh, when he had offered up prayers and supplications with vehement cries and tears to him who was able to save him from death"[191] and not again "to save him from the wrath of God."

Since a personified God, alone, could foresee, and foresense, and foretaste, the extreme pains of death by crucifixion, Christ said, "My soul is exceedingly sorrowful even to death."[192] And "Now my soul is troubled."[193] As "his sweat became like great drops of blood falling down to the ground."[194]

Likewise, his painful complaint and cry on the cross with loud voice, saying, "Eli, Eli, lama Shabach-tani?" Which means, "My God,

---

[190]-*The Twelve. By Leslie B. Flynn. Victor Books. 4th printing 1985, Page 52.*

[191]-*(Hebrews 5:7)*

[192]-*(Mark 14:34)*

[193]-*(John 12:27)*

[194]-*(Luke 22:44)*

My God, why have you forsaken me?"[195] were indeed the last cry and complaint of "the flesh" because of the atrocious pains by crucifixion; for Scripture says here too, "The flesh is weak."[196] Yet, Christ Jesus, the Son, and the Second hypostasis in the Holy Trinity, even while on the cross, was constantly and continuously with the Father and the Holy Spirit: "And yet I am not alone, because the Father is with me."[197]

Now, as for the descent of Christ into "the lower parts of earth,"[198] it was not, God forbid, that there, (I quote only): "The fire and the brimstone that consumed Sodom and Gomorrah fall upon him as the sin bearer of the world," and "that innocent substitute who was now consumed by the molten lava of the wrath of God." But rather, he descended willingly and for the sole purpose of preaching "to the spirits in prison,"[199] and as the very

---

[195]-(Matthew 27:46 and Mark 15:34)

[196]-(Matthew 26:41)

[197]-(John 16:32)

[198]-(Ephesians 4:9)

[199]-(1 Peter 3:19)

Savior[200] and the very Conqueror, and the very Victor as well.[201]

Now, to paraphrase and clear all that with brief explanatory and somewhat illustrative way I say:

Since the Word, or God, "became flesh,[202] without losing or ceding his divinity or deity (from birth, to death, and to resurrection) and came to the world as the very "Lamb of God", a lamb " without blemish" or spot or stain or sin;

Since he came in the form of man, i.e. in the likeness of a sinner (for every man, according to the Scriptures, is a sinner); He, himself was, without sin. He was even baptized in the likeness of a sinner. (All that he did, to accomplish all righteousness;[203] without being, himself, an unrighteous man. For even as a babe of eight days, he was circumcised according to the law, and was called Jesus i.e. the Savior);

---

[200]-*(Hebrews 11:13-16)*

[201]-*(1 Corinthians 15:55)*

[202]-*(John 1:14)*

[203]-*(Matthew 3:15)*

Although by his embodiment, he became even "lower than the angels;"[204] yet the angels did not stop serving and ministering him as their Lord and God;[205]

And though he took "the form of a servant,"[206] he never ceased to be the Almighty God and Lord of the world.

Since he used to sit and eat with sinners and tax-collectors, he was labeled as gluttonous, wine-bibber, and friend of sinners.[207]

Since he was unjustly judged and crucified, (always according to his own will), without being guilty of any sort of sin or crime or the like (As even his betrayers Judas and the criminal on the cross themselves testified according to Matthew 27:4 and Luke 23:41); and because according to Deuteronomy 21:22,23, "If a man has committed a sin worthy of death, and he is put to death. . .(hanged). . . on a tree. . . he is accursed of God", the apostle Paul said metaphorically, "he became a curse

---

[204]-*(Hebrews 2:7 and Psalm 8:5)*

[205]-*(Matthew 4:11 and Mark 1:13)*

[206]-*(Philippians 2:7)*

[207]-*(Matthew 11:19 and Luke 7:34)*

for us"[208] and God "made him who knew no sin to be sin for us."[209] Meaning, "a propitiation for our sins"[210] and not at all, God forbid, guilty of any sort of sin, as some do infer unfairly and that he endured the wrath of God. For the death that he died, (and not the "wrath of God he suffered") he died to sin once for all;"[211] as the embodiment that he embodied, "in the likeness of sinful flesh on account of sin: He condemned sin in the flesh."[212]

Thus, Christ punished sin on the cross, and not as says Spurgeon, "God. . . (punished) sin in Christ."[213] For, God forbid, how can God punish sin or Satan in himself? Isn't such inference infernal indeed? He rather, condemned and punished sin in the seeming and seeing and sinless human body he bore, and not in himself as God or Christ or Son of God or Son of Man.

---

[208]-(Galatians 3:13)

[209]-(2 Corinthians 5:21)

[210]-(1 John 2:2)

[211]-(Romans 6:10)

[212]-(Romans 8:3)

[213]-Spurgeon's Sermons, Volume 2. Page 333.

And to see all that clearly, come compare with me, dear reader, this unbiblical portrait of Christ-God "enduring the wrath of God and the equivalent of eternity in hell" or this "consumed Christ" "by the molten lava of the wrath of God" yes, come and compare all that with his very and pure portrait according to Scriptures themselves as quoted briefly and brilliantly by the Syrian poet and theologian Jacob of Serugh (4th Century):

> The Almighty rose from the tomb with great power.
> Trembling, marveling, the prophet approached and said to him,
> "Lord, why is your apparel red, your side stabbed, and your hands pierced?"
> "I have trodden the winepress in hell mightily,
> And waged the war alone, and weltered in blood,
> Halleluiah! And have risen with glory."

THE DOCTRINE OF SELF-ESTEEM

-1-

[No, it is neither conceivable nor reasonable that God creates equal or identical persons to him as omnipotent, as omniscient, and as omnipresent. Otherwise they would have been a plurality of Gods, and ipso facto, an annihilation of Godhead or Godhood.

Therefore, God created angels less pure and less perfect than him, not only by grade but also by nature. He created them "spirits, servants, and flame of fire."[214] So that they had free will to adore him or not, to obey him or not, and even to rebel against him.

Therefore, due to imperfection of his nature, and because of his free will, the archangel Lucifer rebelled against his Creator. The question here is: But how did it happen, this first rebellion against God? Did Lucifer (with his hosts) wage a war in heavens, as in the Greek mythology and Hesiod's theogony?

---

[214]-(Hebrews 1:7)

Or did he plot a revolt, or a coup d'etat against God? No, absolutely not. It is only because Lucifer thought evil against Him. For as says Jesus "Out of the heart proceeds evil things."[215] It is because Lucifer said in his heart "I will ascend into heavens. I will exalt my throne above the stars of God. . . I will be like the Most High."[216] At that very fraction of moment, he, Lucifer or Satan, fell "like lightning from heaven" as says Jesus to his disciples "I saw Satan fall like lightning from heaven."[217]

For who else but Jesus Christ, who created Lucifer even before the creation of the cosmos, could foresee the evil thoughts of his heart, and see his fatal fall in consequence?

Then, with the fall of Lucifer, called now Satan, evil entered the world for the first time, and with evil sin and death, through the first sinner, man, as Paul says in Romans.[218]

Oh how sinful and disastrous are the evil thoughts of man! They are sometimes more grievous, more horrendous, and even more

---

[215]-*(Matthew 16:19)*

[216]-*(Isaiah 14:13,14)*

[217]-*(Luke 10:18)*

[218]-*(Rom 5:12)*

harmful than the evil deeds themselves. Isn't it because of the sin of the heart, or of the mind, that the Apostle Paul cried bitterly, "O wretched man that I am! Who will deliver me from this body of death? I thank God -through Jesus Christ our Lord!"[219] And David declared desperately, "In sin did my mother conceive me."[220]

It is said that Jesus appeared to a certain ascetic, and handed him a loaf of bread to give to the greatest sinner he ever heard about. "Tomorrow, he said to him, I will be back to find out your final decision." The next day Jesus saw him eating the bread. Asked, the ascetic explained saying, "Lord and God, I dared not give it even to Judas Iscariot who betrayed you for thirty denarii, nor to Peter who denied you thrice, nor to David who robbed Uriah's wife and murdered him. And because you urged us saying, "Judge not, that you be not judged". Besides, Lord and Gracious God, the sins of these servants of yours are well known. Whereas mine, to you alone are revealed, and they do put me to shame even to death indeed."

Thus, the more a Christian grows in righteousness, the more sensitive to sin he

---

[219]-(Romans 7:24,25)

[220]-(Psalms 61:5)

137

becomes, and the more tempted by "all that is in the world -the lust of the flesh, the lust of the eyes, and the pride of life."[221] And the more he senses the sting of sin, and feels that he is a great sinner, the more also he is prone to perfection, rather he has penchant to remorse and repentance in order to be more perfect, "Just as (His) Father in heaven is perfect."[222]

St. Ephrem, (4th Century) "The harp of the Holy Spirit," "The sun of the Syrians," the ascetic, the scholar, the teacher and preacher of the Gospel, the great commentator on the Bible, the prophet, and the poet who wrote around three million verses about biblical topics according to Hayes (In his book: The History of Edessa-In French) St. Ephrem says in his noted death bed Testament:

"In vanities and sins I spent my life and hours.
Whoever showed you my trespasses, all of you would spit on my face.
For, if the smell of my sins has spread, no one could approach me."

---

[221]-(1 John 2:16)

[222]-(Matthew 5:48)

138

Although "A chosen vessel of God," as called by Christ himself,[223] and "Caught up to the third heaven. . . into paradise,"[224] even the Apostle Paul, the very architect of Christendom, does contend testifying to Timothy, "This is a faithful saying and worthy of all acceptance, that Christ Jesus came to the world to save sinners of whom I am chief."[225]

Thus, the keen sense of sin, is not at all "a sense of shame and unworthiness,"[226] but on the contrary, a continuous contrition and compensation, sublimity and spiritualization that lead to that great satisfaction and exaltation, rather to that very "joy in heart" that no one will rob from the faithful.[227]

But, to have no sense of sin at all, or deny daringly the very existence of sin, is to sin constantly and consciously;[228] to live and die,

---

[223]-*(Acts 9:15)*

[224]-*(2 Corinthians 12:2,4)*

[225]-*(1 Timothy 1:15)*

[226]-*Self-Esteem. The New Reformation. by Robert H. Schuller. A Jove Book. Jove edition/November 1985. (The Introduction. Page 14)*

[227]-*(John 16:22)*

[228]-*(Romans 1:18-21)*

thereby, in sin consequently, and to be damned and doomed eternally indeed. "For the wages of sin is death."[229]][230]

-2-

Jean Jacque Rousseau (18th Century), the French philosopher, believed that "man, by nature, is good; but it is society that deprives him." And the World Book Encyclopedia sums up his philosophy in this respect; "He felt that when people lived in a state of nature, isolated and without language, they were good - that is, they had no motive or impulse to hurt one another. But as soon as they began to live together in society, they became evil."[231]

Somehow, secular humanists or humanitarianists, including certain religious leaders, reject the basic and biblical teaching that every man is born in sinful state.

For instance, Pinhas Lapide, the Orthodox Jewish German theologian, although taking somehow the same standing as Rousseau vis-a-vis the pseudo-goodness of man, he,

---

[229]-*(Romans 6:23 and Genesis 3:3)*

[230]-*From Orthodox Fathers, Orthodox Faith.*

[231]-*World Book, Inc. A Scott Fetzer Company. Copyright 1983, U.S.A.*

however, ascribes it to Scriptures themselves. Says Lapide, "Judaism does not believe in redemption from the world the way Paul (the apostle Paul) does, (No, Paul does not believe in redemption <u>from</u> <u>the</u> <u>world</u>, but rather from sin, original sin) but rather believes in the ultimate reconciliation of all earthly discord and duality (Lapide does use here Paul's somehow same or similar statement in Colossians 1:20; "And by Him to reconcile all things to Him, by Him, whether things on earth or things in heaven etc.), and because of its incorrigible optimism which begins on the very first page of the Bible where six times God pronounces the whole creation "good" and refers to human beings, the bearers of his image as "very good", Judaism reposes its faith in the intrinsic value of God's world."[232]

Yes indeed, at the very beginning "the whole creation was good;" as Adam and Eve were created "very good," and even while naked, "they were not ashamed."[233] But after the Temptation and Fall of Man, sin and evil entered the world, and deformed and defiled

---

[232]-*Paul Rabbi and Apostle. Origin German edition copyright 1981. Calwer Verlag, Stuttgart, and Kosel-Verlag GmbH & Co., Munich. English language edition copyright 1984 Angslung Publishing. Minneapolis. Pp. 46,47.*

[233]-*(Genesis 2:25)*

man's pure image that was made "in God's image, according to His likeness."[234]

Here, it is Moses himself, the very author and writer of Genesis by inspiration of God, who depicts in dramatic, drastic, and decisive terms the very "wickedness" (and not "goodness") of man, and his "continuous evilness" as well, saying, "Then the Lord God saw that the <u>wickedness</u> of man was great in the earth, and that <u>every</u> <u>intent</u> <u>of</u> <u>the</u> <u>thoughts</u> <u>of</u> <u>his</u> <u>heart</u> <u>was</u> <u>only</u> <u>evil</u> <u>continuously</u>."[235]

Then after Moses, and always by inspiration of God, many prophets of the Torah echoed the very "wickedness" of man and not again, his very "goodness" at all, as the following instances indicate:

David, who even though a man "after God's own heart,"[236] yet, his very heart was not clean at all, so that he earnestly besought God to "create in him a clean heart."[237] As he didn't

---

[234]-*(Genesis 1:26)*

[235]-*(Genesis 6:5)*

[236]-*(1 Samuel 13:14 and Acts 13:22)*

[237]-*(Psalm 52:10)*

142

even refrain from declaring, "And in sin my mother conceived me."[238]

And Isaiah, proclaimed generalizing, "But we <u>are</u> <u>all</u> like unclean things, and <u>all</u> our righteousness are like filthy rags..."[239]

And Jeremiah said categorically, "The heart is deceitful above all things, and desperately wicked; who can know it?"[240]

If so, where is then the "very goodness" of man in all this? How come, again, Pinhas Lapide accuses Paul, saying, "...he invented an un-Jewish affliction - original sin - in order to cure it with an anti-Jewish remedy - a human sacrifice which serves as an atoning death. . . he transformed the optimistic view of creation recorded in Genesis, which portrays human beings as good, into a pessimistic Hellenistic view which considers humans by nature too sinful and weak to be worthy of salvation without God's grace, and so on and so forth?"[241]

---

[238]-(Psalm 51:5)

[239]-(Isaiah 64:6)

[240]-(Jeremiah 17:9)

[241]-Ibid. Page 53

2

It seems to me, that Dr. and Rev. Robert H. Schuller assumes almost the same and similar secular stand like Rousseau and Lapide towards the pseudo-goodness of men and original sin (in his book Self-Esteem: The New Reformation). Reports Time Magazine, March 18, 1985, "For Schuller, an acknowledgement of self-worth, more than a confession of sinfulness, is the path of God. He says, "We can replace inferiority complex with a new self-image, one with divine roots. God is my Father, I am somebody."

Even though Schuller is convinced "that the deepest of all human needs is salvation from sin and hell. I see sin in all-pervasive in humanity, infecting all human behavior and polluting the social institutions and systems at every level. The result of sin is death and hell;"[242] he, however, does not consider sin a rebellion against God, while the Apostle Paul does assert, "For as by one man's disobedience many were made sinners. . .[243] To Schuller, "sin is that deep lack of trust that separates me from God and leaves me with a sense of shame and unworthiness," or "sin is any act or thought

---

[242]-*Self-Esteem: The Introduction*

[243]-*(Romans 5:19)*

that robs myself or another human being of his or her self-esteem."[244]

Then, daringly and, rather defiantly, Schuller proclaims "Classical theology defines sin as "rebellion against God." The answer is not incorrect as much as it is shallow and insulting to the human being."[245]

Now, if sin was not a "disobedience" or a rebellion against God because of the rejecting and breaking of his commandments in the past, as "continuously", why then "the wages of sin is death?"[246] i.e. eternal and total perdition and expulsion from the presence of God?

And if sin, as proclaims Schuller, was a simple "lack of trust" or a main "inferiority complex with which we are all born"[247] why again its consequences would be this severe punishment in hell? For it is Schuller himself, here too, who admits emphatically, saying, "I am convinced that the deepest of all human needs is salvation from sin in hell?"

---

[244]-*Self-Esteem: The Introduction*

[245]-*Ibid. Page 65*

[246]-*(Romans 6:23)*

[247]-*Ibid. Page 65*

Says Schuller, "Yes, what we need in the World Wide Christian Church, (As if there are also "in the world wide" Jewish and Moslem and Buddhist Churches!) is nothing less than a new reformation. Where the sixteenth century Reformation returned our focus to Sacred Scriptures as the only infallible rule for faith and practice, the new reformation (i.e. his reformation) will return our focus to the sacred right of every person to self-esteem! The fact is, the church will never succeed until it satisfies the human being's hunger for self-value."[248]

Thus, this "This what we need" repeated time and again in his book, will be its leitmotif from cover to cover for the sole salvation of self-esteem, or self-value, or self-pride, or self-dignity, or self-worth and so forth, and so on, of every person.

As if the sacred Scriptures themselves scorn, or spurn, negate, neglect, or reject, deny, or denounce, undervalue, or underestimate "the sacred right of every person to self-esteem!

As if, Dr. and Rev. Robert Schuller alone, is the only preacher and paladin, patron and champion, defender and fighter, expounder and mentor, advocator and sole savior of self-value of every individual!

---

[248]-*Ibid. Page 38*

Isn't Paul, himself who two thousand years before Schuller, taught and preached diligently to respect and protect man's dignity and self-esteem as a very child of God, saying, "The Spirit himself bears witness with our spirit, that <u>we</u> <u>are</u> <u>children</u> <u>of</u> <u>God,</u> <u>and</u> <u>if</u> <u>children,</u> <u>then</u> <u>heirs</u> - <u>heirs</u> <u>with</u> <u>him</u> <u>(Christ)</u> that we may also be glorified together."[249] And to the Galatians writes Paul, "And because you are sons, God has sent forth the Spirit of His Son into your hearts, crying out, "Abba, Father!" Therefore you are no longer a slave but a son, and if a son, then an heir of God through Christ"[250] etc. etc.

Now, what more stress and emphasis on human dignity, worth, value, and "self-esteem, do you need" than all those stupendous statements of Paul that make man, not only a gentleman endowed and adorned with pride and glory and self-worth, but furthermore, a very son of God, and legitimate heir with Christ himself, "The Lord of glory," in the inheritance of his heavenly Kingdom?

Isn't Paul again and again, who, writing to the Corinthians, declares, "Do you not know that your body is the temple of the Holy Spirit

---

[249]-*(Romans 8:16,17)*

[250]-*(Galatians 4:6,7)*

147

who is in you, whom you have from God, and you are not your own?"[251] etc. etc. etc.

But, what really alarms and disheartens is that Dr. Robert Schuller, is not only sacrificing the sacred Scripture for the sacred right of every person to self-esteem, but rather he is rejecting them for being "the only infallible rule for faith and practice!"

-3-

Schuller's claim that "Adam's children were born detached from a trusting relationship with heavenly Father. Their lives unlike their father's started out not knowing God"[252] totally contradicts the sacred Scriptures. For Moses himself says here too "The men (just after Adam begot Seth and Seth begot Enoch" i.e. Adam's very children) began to call on the name of the Lord."[253] Even Cain and Abel, Adam's first and foremost two sons, knew God well; both of them brought their offerings to God: Cain's, "the fruit of ground", and Abel's, "the firstlings of his flock."[254] And that of course, by advice and guidance of their parents.

---

[251]-(1 Corinthians 6:9)

[252]-Ibid. Page 14

[253]-(Genesis 5:25,26)

[254]- (Genesis 4:3,4)

148

And by his other claim that Adam's children "were born in the jungle, disconnected, alienated, out-of-touch. Since then, all of us were born nontrusting creatures of the jungle,"[255] Schuller is again and again contradicting Moses himself that says about Adam's children that they used to "till the ground," build cities, dwell in tents and have livestock," and "play the harp and flute;" as they were instructors "of every craftsman in bronze and iron."[256]

Thus, whereas the sacred Scriptures do maintain that man, from the very outset, was supernaturally created and drastically distinct from all other living creatures, was made "in God's own image, according to His likeness,"[257] the other "living creatures were created each according to its "very kind;"[258] Schuller, by claiming that "Adam's children were born in the jungle, disconnected etc. etc.", is advocating thereby, and willy-nilly, the atheistic revolutionary and philosophical theory that teaches that man evolved from an ape about a span of 30 to 70 million years ago or the like.

---

[255]-*Ibid. Page 65*

[256]-*(Genesis 4:12,17,20,21,22)*

[257]-*(Genesis 1:26)*

[258]-*(Genesis 6)*

Self-Esteem: The New Reformation, is rife and replete with such unbiblical and unprecedented statements that I picked up at random. I would like to mention and comment on the final following ones:

Schuller says, "Christ is the Word made flesh. Christ is the Lord over the Scriptures; the Scriptures are not Lord over Christ."[259] The spontaneous response to such statements is: These are sophistry and unbiblical words. For the divine power of Christ is expressed in his very teaching. And to belittle or deprecate the Scriptures, is to minimize Christ himself who said, "If you love me, keep my commandments."[260] For as Christ is "the life"[261] likewise the "words" that he speaks "are spirit and life."[262]

Thus, he deprived Christ from his commandments or the Scriptures. For although God in the Old Testament spoke through the Scriptures, it is through Christ or the Word that

---

[259]-*Ibid. Page 45.*

[260]-*(John 14:15)*

[261]-*(John 11;25 and 14:6)*

[262]-*(John 6:63)*

150

God was revealed, known, and seen thoroughly, plainly and absolutely.

This is a new wave of the new age, a treacherous and brazen attempt to rule out and sap the Scriptures themselves.

Dr. Robert Schuller also says, "We are saved by the "blood" not by the "Book."[263] Again it is another aberration if not apostasy. It is his lively and revolutionary teachings, and his "new commandment" that is "love;"[264] and particularly of his claim of being God and Son of God, that Christ Jesus was crucified,[265] his blood shed, and in consequence, we have been saved by his blood. For, if "they (the rulers of the age and religious leaders) had known (i.e. that Christ Jesus was God himself) they would not have crucified the Lord of glory."[266]

Jesus Christ is metaphorically his Blood and his Book combined. And he who rejects his Book that teaches that Christ became flesh for our salvation[267] or diminish or degrade or

---

[263]-*Ibid. Page 45*

[264]-*(John 13:34)*

[265]-*(Matthew 26;64-66 and Mark 14;61-64)*

[266]-*(1 Corinthians 2:7,8)*

[267]-*(John 1:14)*

debase his Book beneath him, can by no means be saved by his blood alone. For his blood is shed for those who <u>love</u> <u>him</u> and keep his commandments.

Dr. Robert Schuller further says, "We believe in the holy Trinity, not a holy Quadrangle."[268] What a gibberish! What a gobbledegook! For again, where is the slightest relationship between the first sentence: "We believe in the holy Trinity", and the second absurd and ridiculous one; "not a holy Quadrangle?" His purpose is clear, mock the Scriptures, and to debunk the sacred. It is to ridicule even the holy Trinity, and make thereby his audience laugh and be impressed by his wordily wit and sophistry?

-5-

Now the crucial question here is: Why Schuller's audiences and readers seem, somehow, to be very easy prey to his charm and charisma, so to speak?

Seers, soothsayers, and fortune-tellers of pre-Islamic times used to captivate individuals and masses with their rhyming and precise prose. And to convince and convert antique Arabs enamored of poetry (rhymed poetry), the

---

[268]-*Ibid. Page 45*

Quran's Surats (or verses) were delivered in turn, somewhat, with rhyming prose, and seducing sound of poetic jingle.

In like manner, fourteen centuries later, Dr. and Rev. Robert Schuller, the Televangelist and stylist, is delivering his sensational series of sermons and publications. Yes, with imitative harmony, rhyming slogans, rhythmical and resounding terms and terminologies (Somehow also like his paradigm Dr. Norman Vincent Peale, but with more affected style), he touches the sensitive spots of his followers, hits their eardrums, and captivates their poor souls.

From his book Self-Esteem: The New Reformation, I quote the following:

"...to merge mind, motive, method and message" (Page 30)
"...are premium persons, not peasant or paws" (Page 63)
"...Our natural fears take the face and form and force of anger" (Page 66)

"It sets a self-esteem-setting standard for his sacred society" (Page 74) - Notice here the 11 successive Ss+c in one single sentence).

-...by doing his work, by walking his walk and by following his will our work must be our worship (Page 94) - another 8 successive sounds of "Ws" in one sentence.

153

-To discover their self-worth through salvation and subsequent social service in our Savior's name (Page 118) (Notice here too the 8 successive Ss in one sentence).

-We must be friendly and fair as well as frank and firm (Page 132). And so on and so forth from cover to cover.

And from the "The Be (Happy) Attitudes"[269] (This title seems to be inspired by "happy attitudes" in the following sentence, "start each day by affirming peaceful contended, and happy attitudes etc." of Schuller's "early model Positive Thinker Norman Vincent Peal," in his book entitled "The Power of Positive Thinking)[270] I quote the following:

-...Sorrow will change our tomorrow (Page 49)
-...Good people turn their scars into stars (Page 69)
-...How do you handle your hidden wounds? Don't nurse them. Don't curse them. Don't release them. Do immerse them. And finally reverse them. (Page 142) etc. etc.

---

[269]-*World Books. Publisher Waco, Texas. Copyright 1985.*

[270]-*Prentice Hall Press-New York-Special 35th Anniversary Edition. Copyright 1987. Page 22.*

Time Magazine, March 18, 1985 puts it this way, "Schuller speaks earnestly of the abiding desire for self-worth, of "every person's deepest need - one's spiritual hunger with a smorgasbord of rhyming slogans: "There's no gain without pain," "It takes guts to leave the ruts."

And Time, February 17, 1986, to put it this other way, "Schuller's sermons, taxing to neither spirit nor intellect, awe as much to psychology as to Scripture. They are peppered with greeting-card aphorisms for seekers of happiness and self-esteem." Coping and hoping." "Turn your scars into stars." The cross is "a minus turned into a plus."

Furthermore, by cramming constantly his followers with crumbs of jocular commentaries and his continuous publications, a farrago of scriptural and secular statements, he is giving them no respite, neither to read, nor to revise the Scriptures, lest they perceive the drastic difference between his bizarre beliefs and teachings, and what the Bible says.

And not least of all, why Schuller's persistent and pseudo-purpose for the saving of self-esteem that is already well sound, safe, and saved by Christ alone and keeping his commandment?

If not, yes, in the sole purpose, pretext, and plea to please (using his smorgasbord of rhyming slogans) always his audiences and readers, even through anti-Scriptural, and stereotype statements, and sardonic slogans as: "We believe in the Holy Trinity not a holy Quadrangle" and the like?

If not, then, in the sole goal to attack even the sacred, so that to attract more attention, more recognition, and, alas, more ephemeral fame and vain glory even from Non-Christians and from nominal Christian alike?

If not, to gain, without real pain, more money, always more money, for the establishing of his earthly kingdom handed from father to son, and grandsons as well?

And if not so again, why Time Magazine March 18, 1985 does report as doubtful, "Schuller, 58, a self-described retailer of religion and apostle of possibility thinking is probably the most controversial religious figure in American Protestantism" and "The question, Vosquil (Religious Historian Dennis Vosquil) says, is whether he (Schuller) will be remembered as a Theologian or a showman?" And why Rev. Billy Graham himself labels, very skillfully, Schuller's ministry as "An amazing ministry?" (See the back flap of "Self-Esteem: The New Reformation". For what is more amazing, doubtful, and dreadful than Schuller's

156

successive statements and slogans that, not only contradict the Bible, but rather offend it directly, daringly, and systematically?

-6-

Paul's inspired declaration that Christ "made Himself of no reputation, taking the form of a servant. . . (and) humbled Himself and became obedient to the point of death, even the death of the cross"[271] is now explained by Robert Schuller, in the context of today's success-oriented world, to mean:

"Jesus knew his worth, his success fed his self-esteem. . . He suffered the cross to sanctify his self-esteem. And he bore the cross to sanctify your self-esteem.

"And the cross will sanctify the ego trip (emphasis in the original!)

"Success and self-esteem have become so important in the Church that they seem to overshadow everything else."[272]

---

[271]-*(Philippians 2:7,8)*

[272]-*The Seduction of Christianity. By Dave Hunt & T.A. McMahon. Harvest House Publishers. Eugene, Oregon 97402. Copyright 1985. Pp. 14,15.*

Returning from a visit to Rome, our late Patriarch Ignatius Jacob III, was reporting about his visit to the Vatican. He was telling his large audience exultantly, how differences between Catholicism and Orthodoxy exist no more, and how Pope Paul VI welcomed him as his very equal by calling him "Holiness;" and how, while outside his residency, he broke even the protocol for the first time by descending seven steps to bid him farewell.

That was, in fact and undeniably an unprecedented, unpredictable, and proper gesture on the part of a Pope, since centuries, toward our Syrian Church represented by our Patriarch.

But to me, Christian values as holiness and humbleness, humility and meekness were above all else. Therefore, I couldn't restrain myself at that solemn moment. I was sitting at the far end of the reception room just in front of our Patriarch. And of course, without intending to hurt his feelings, (He was a famous scholar, historian, hagiographer, and author of more than thirty publications till that time) I addressed him saying, as if I didn't hear his last words, "How many stairs did his Holiness descend?" "Seven," he retorted, not expecting my daring and direct reply: "But, Sayyedna" (our Rabbi, in Arabic), I blurted out, "how many seven sevens did Christ descend from the heavens, not only to greet or bid farewell to man whom he created, but to also wash his feet, even the feet of the very one who will betray him? Humility, Rabbi, should emit and emanate particularly from you, Popes you are or Patriarchs, Prelates or Potentates."

Oh! I never ever forgave myself for such a daring remark on that solemn Sunday! For I could have said it to him in privacy. I wasn't Paul who rebuked Peter openly.[273] I didn't even apologize to him after that. Besides, while young, he was (before being ordained a monk) my tutor and teacher of catechism, a close friend to my father. Thereafter (as an Archbishop then a Patriarch) I became in turn his close friend. Therefore, now only, while penning this chapter, I do apologize with Paul, "You shall not offend the ruler of your people."[274] May his soul in paradise forgive me.

By the way, isn't it Wisdom that says, "Pride, and arrogance, and the evil way, and the perverse mouth, I hate?"[275]

---

[273]-(Galatians 2:14)

[274]-(Acts 23:5)

[275]-(Proverbs 8:13)

THE DOCTRINE OF MILLENNIUM

-1-

To deal with Millennium or the supposed Kingdom of God Christ on earth for one thousand years, we have, first, to evaluate Revelation or the Apocalypse attributed to the Apostle John (the last book of the New Testament, and the only one, that somehow, treats this subject).

Perhaps the book of Revelation (written most probably around the year 90 AD) was revealed, once and for all, to his author only. It was also disclosed to him alone the plot and treason of Judas Iscariot.[276]

Until now, this book did not disclose its full state, secret, and mysteries to two persons identically or similarly. And this, because most of its visions and images are rife with signs, and replete with symbols. Its allegorical values and

---

[276]-*(John 13:26)*

views, are made up, mostly of metaphors, figures, pictures, persons, animals, things, names, numbers, and body's members. The number "seven" per se, is "adopted generally as a cyclical number, with the subordinate notions of perfection or complements."[277]

This specific number "seven," for instance, is repeated often, more than seventeen times successively, almost in seventeen chapters, as follows:

-The seven Churches and seven Spirits (1:4)
-The seven golden lampstands (2:1)
-The seven Spirits of God and the seven stars (3:1)
-Seven lamps of fire (4:5)
-Seven seals (5:1)
-Seven horns and seven eyes which are the seven Spirits of God (5:6)
-Seven angels and the seven trumpets (8:2)
-Seven hundreds uttered their voices (10:3)
-Seven thousand men (11:13)
-Seven heads and seven diadems (12:3)
-Seven Angels (15:1)
-Seven golden bowls (15:8)
-Seven heads and seven mountains (17:9)

---

[277]-*Smith's Bible Dictionary. By William Smith, L.L.D.*

Thus, because of the difficulty, rather the impossibility of comprehending and interpreting the diverse symbols (that embrace diverse facts, occurring in diverse times, throughout the unknown early or further future as well) our prime and primitive Church in Christendom, did not dare include the book of Revelation among the canonical Scriptures till the fifth century.

About the liturgical use of Revelation in the Church, says the Orthodox Study Bible, "While seen as canonical and inspired by God, Revelation is the only New testament book not publicly read in the services of the Orthodox Church. This is partly because the book was only gradually accepted as canonical in many parts in Christendom."[278]

It will be proper to point out here, that even Eusebius (260 A.D.) "the father of ecclesiastical history - the first, the only historian of the church bordering on primitive times"[279] as it seems, places the book of Revelation among spurious books. He writes:

---

[278]-*Orthodox Study Bible, page 589.*

[279]-*Eusebius. The History of the Church from Christ to Constantine. Translated by F.A. Williamson. Augsburg Publishing House. Minneapolis, Minnesota. Copyright 1965. (The Introduction Page 7.)*

"It will be well, at this point, to classify the New Testament writings already referred to. We must, of course, put first the holy quarter of the gospels, followed by the Acts of the Apostles. The next place in the list goes to Paul's epistles, and after them we must recognize the epistle called 1 John; likewise 1 Peter. To these may be added if it is thought proper, the Revelation of John, the arguments about which I shall set out when the time comes. These are classed as Recognized Books. Those that are disputed, yet familiar to most, include the epistles known as James, Jude, and 2 Peter, and those called 2 and 3 John, the work either of the evangelist or of someone else with the same name.

Among spurious books must be placed the "Acts" of Paul, the "Shepherd", and the "Revelation of Peter;" also the alleged "Epistle of Barnabas", and the "Teachings of the Apostles", together with the Revelation of John, if this seems the right place for it: as I said before,, some reject it, others include it among the Recognized Books."[280]

Later, about the so-called Kingdom of Christ on earth for one thousand years," it is always Eusebius, under the title "The Ebionite sect: the heresies of Cerinthus and Nicolaus"[281]

---

[280]-*Ibid. Page 134.*

[281]-*Ibid. Page 136.*

who states that "At the time under discussion, tradition tells us, another heretical sect was founded by Cerinthus (A Judaizing gnostic). Gaius, whose words I quoted earlier, in the Disputation attributed to him writes this about him: "Then there is Cerinthus, who by revelations purporting to have been written by a great apostle presents us with the tales of wonder falsely alleged to have been shown to him by angels. He declares that after the Resurrection, the Kingdom of Christ will be on earth, and that carnal humanity will dwell in Jerusalem, once more enslaved to lusts and pleasures. And in his enmity towards the Scriptures of God, and his anxiety to lead men astray, he foretells a period of a thousand years given up to wedding festivities."[282]

Then, referring to Dionysius (third Century) the bishop of Alexandria, Eusebius does continue, saying:

"Dionysius again, who held the bishopric of the Alexandrian see in my own time, in Book 2 of his Promises, makes certain statements about the Revelation of John on the basis of very ancient tradition. He then refers to Cerinthus in the following terms: "Cerinthus; the founder of a sect called Cerinthian after him; who wished to attach a name commanding respect to his own creation. This, they say, was

---

[282]-*Ibid. Page 138.*

the doctrine he taught that Christ's Kingdom would be on earth; and the things he lusted after himself, being the slave of his body and sensual through and through, filled the heaven of his dreams-unlimited indulgence in gluttony and lechery at banquets, drinking-bouts, and wedding-feasts, or (to call these by what he thought more respectable names) festivals, sacrifices, and the immolation of victims."[283]

Michael the Great, the Syrian historian and the patriarch of Antioch (1166-1199) writing about the Apocalypse, or the book of Revelations, says: "Eusebius says that the Apocalypse of John is not of the Apostle, but of John the Priest, or of Cerinthe who used to teach that the Elect will eat and drink on earth. It is admitted that it is in this way; for the style of the Apocalypse does not resemble that of the Gospel and the Epistle (of John). And because John the Evangelist does not put at all his name in these books as it is inserted in this one (The Apocalypse), and also because the author was not familiar with the Greek language, but he uses from time to time, a barbarous language."[284]

---

[283]-Ibid. Page 138.

[284]-Chronique de Michel Le Syrian, Patriarche Jacobite d'Antioche. Traduite en Francais par J.B. Chabot. Paris 1898. Culture et Civilisation 115. Avenues Gabriel Lebon. Bruxelles 1963. Tome 1, Livre 6. Chapitre 9; Pages 198-199.

Four centuries later, Martin Luther (1483-1546), the father of the Reformation, "at first, (says Durant) rates the Apocalypse as an unintelligible farrago of promises and threats, neither Apostolic nor Prophetic."[285]

-2-

No, I personally, cannot deny the very veracity, or authenticity, or the spiritual character of the Book of Revelation. For I do believe that "all Scripture is given by inspiration of God, and is profitable for doctrine, for reproof, for connection, for instruction in righteousness."[286]

Therefore, I do believe, the reading of the Apocalypse is always profitable for the marshaling of Christian moral norms, demeanor, and deportment; as "for instruction in righteousness" as Paul states.

Now, it is obvious that most of the preachers and teachers of the Gospel who herald enthusiastically the so-called "millennial reign of Christ on earth," draw this bizarre belief from the Book of Revelation. And amazingly enough, they draw it particularly and specifically from chapter 20, verses 4 through 8;

---

[285]-*The Story of Civilisation, Simon and Schuster, N.Y. 1917. Part 6; The Reformation in Germany, 7. The Foundation of Faith. Page 370.*

[286]-*(2 Timothy 3:16)*

regardless of the four gospels of Matthew, Mark, Luke and John; and of the entire epistles of the apostles, and, of twenty centuries of Church tradition, that did not brandish such a belief, that might be symbolic too in the book of Revelation.

I think it will be useful to quote here the above mentioned chapter 20 of Revelation with its five verses: "And I saw thrones, and they sat on them, and judgement was committed to them. And I saw the souls of those who had been beheaded for their witness to Jesus and for the word of God, who had not worshipped the beast or his image, and had not received his mark on their foreheads or on their hands. And they lived and reigned with Christ for a thousand years. But the rest of the dead did not live again until the thousand years were finished. This is the first resurrection.
Blessed and holy is he who has past in the first resurrection. Over such the second death has no power, but they shall be priests of God and of Christ, and shall reign with Him a thousand years. Now when the thousand years have expired, Satan will be released from his prison, and will go out to deceive the nations which are in the four corners of the earth, Gog and Magog, to gather them together to battle, whose number is as the sand of the sea."[287]

---

[287]-(Revelation 20:4-8)

What truly astonishes me, is the pretention of those preachers and teachers of the Gospel, that they have solved all the secrets, signs, and symbols of the Apocalypse.

And what does alarm me more, their audacity, rather their daredeviltry of brandishing thereby almost every day, the threats and menaces of this Book, to frighten, credulous Christians.

If not so, why then prod and provoke nations to wage wars against other nations? Isn't their purpose to draw nearer the End of the Age, as if fate and future of peoples were in their own hands? Or to fulfill thereby, at least, their own allegations or their proper pseudo-predictions? Or, as Grace Halsell puts it, "to trigger a war that would not end until we have destroyed Planet Earth through self-fulfilling prophecy."[288]

If not so, why then torment the souls of simple and credulous people by the early coming of trials and tribulations, and the awful visions of the Book of Revelation?

If not so, why then stimulate imaginations by suspense (as in the American movies) and afflict minds by suspicion, and false

---

[288]-*Prophecy And Politics. By Grace Halsell. Lawrence Hill & Company. Westport, Connecticut. Copyright 1986. Page 198.*

and fearful interpretations of the Book of
Revelation?

If not so, why then this continuous
heralding, especially in hectic hours and
dreadful days, (that are somehow natural
everywhere and every time) of the very
imminent coming of Christ, as today is, surely
and certainly, his very Day?

If not so, why then, at last but not least,
trumpeting the Second and Final coming of the
Son of Man, even before "the great sound of
the trumpet?"[289] or before "the last trumpet?"[290]

Is it because the faithful are gullible, or
credulous and generous, or pious, pure in heart,
and thereby easy prey?

Yes, indeed, the faithful are so.

As most false prophets and preachers of
the Gospel are, everywhere and every time,
"ravenous wolves that do not spare the flock;"[291]
and rapacious vultures that devour "widows'

---

[289]-(Matthew 24:31)

[290]-(1 Corinthians 15:52)

[291]-(Acts 20:20)

houses, and for a pretense make long prayers."[292] And special ones also.

All this does remind me of the following funny anecdote: It tales that when America dropped the atomic bomb on Hiroshima, on the sixth of August 1945, and Japan surrendered; it happened, a week later, that a simple and pious young man (in a certain church of the Middle East?) heard the pastor admonishing vehemently from the pulpit: "Believers in Christ, believe me. We are at this very moment, at the very edge of the End of the Age. And this very year, will certainly be the last year in the lifetime of time. For Christ's coming is drawing nigh. He is rather at the doors. Prepare yourselves for his coming and think of nothing else."

The anecdote continues, "our pious and simple man began since then to live, for the first time, lavishly. Meanwhile, as a gesture of repentance and preparation for Christ's close coming, he also distributed gradually, and gratis, all the contents of his store (a grocery) to the poor and the needy. But the war ended, and to no avail he waited for the end of the Age at the very end of that year and long thereafter. Now, forlorn and furious, he rushed to the preacher's house and said to him menacingly shouting, "Listen to me, false

---

[292]-*(Matthew 23:16)*

preacher. The war ended. The year ended. The contents of my store ended; and I see no signs to the End of the Age as you sermonized. Restore my store, or it will be, this time, and indeed the very end of your own life."

The most ironic, almost half a century later, and exactly in April 1988, and while writing this (in America) I personally, received a so-called "Special-Personal invitation" to a certain city, from Rev, Dereck Prince, the so-called "internationally recognized pastor and author", to repeat to me and to other faithful there, (in city X) about the very approach of the Last Days of the World. Of course, and as usual, begging for money for his Everlasting missionary!

No, dear pastors, preachers, authors and actors; again no. The merciful and gracious God will never ever permit his beautiful universe[293] to be exposed, so easily, to the monstrous menaces of pseudo-biblicists and prophets. Anyhow, with threats or without threats, every "wicked and adulterous generation,"[294] and "faithless and perverse generation,"[295] and "sinful generation"[296] will,

---

[293]-(Genesis 1:9 and 1:18 and 1:21 etc.)

[294]-(Matthew 16:4)

[295]-(Matthew 17:17)

sooner or later, pass away, and be doomed, and condemned to eternal death, even before the very coming of the Son of Man.

Besides, God has still many incorrupt cities, much more valuable than Sodom and Gomorrah; and more than "ten" righteous on earth.[297] Man himself that God created in his image, according to his likeness,[298] has in turn more good and marvelous things to create. For, I deem, the more we discover and unravel God's great marvels and mysteries, the more He is godified[299] and glorified. And as his works have been revealed once in a born blind man to whom Christ restored his sight[300] and in Lazarus' sickness and resurrection,[301] as it was revealed scores and scores of times elsewhere, likewise, God was surely glorified when the man, his beloved creature and son, believed in his self-existence and embodiment, set light on the light bulb, and stepped on the moon, etc., etc. Didn't Christ Jesus say, "Truly, truly I say

---

[296]-(Mark 8:38)

[297]-(Genesis 18:32)

[298]-(Genesis 1:26)

[299]-As the verb "deify" deriving from the Latin "deus" or God.

[300]-(John 9:1-7)

[301]-(John 11:4-44)

173

to you he who believes in Me, the works that I do he will do also; and greater works than these he will do."[302]

Now, and according to the Scriptures themselves, wouldn't all Israel be saved before the second coming of Christ?[303] And if so, why then, finally, this premature tumultuous, tempesting, and trumpeting even before that blessing event and very moment?

From a rabid rabbi, we see the Apostle Paul, just after his conversion, pronouncing his immediate proclamation, even in the synagogues, that Christ "is the Son of God;"[304] yes, we see him becoming a compassionate Christian. He becomes so compassionate, rather much more rabid, especially vis-a-vis his people Israel. For, although to him "to live is Christ,"[305] yet he does wish so earnestly that "he himself was accursed-namely denying Christ and dying as a damned-for his brethren, (his) kinsmen according to the flesh, who are Israelites, to whom pertain scriptures, the glory, the covenants, the giving of the Law, the service of God, and the promises; of whom are the

---

[302]-(John 14:12)

[303]-(Romans 11:26)

[304]-(Acts 9:20)

[305]-(Philippians 1:21)

174

Fathers, and from whom according to the flesh, Christ came, who is over all, the eternally blessed God. Amen."[306]

In this so sincere, so loving, and so visionary statement of Paul, isn't his stupendous sacrifice (for his people), although, and especially, mental, moral, and not physical only, the utmost one ever done by a man of God?

Departing, however, from Isaiah prophecy "The Deliverer will come out of Zion and he will turn away ungodliness from Jacob, for this my covenant with them, when I take away their sins,"[307] Paul in turn gives evidence after evidence (at least for instance) in three chapters (9,10,11) of his epistle to the Romans, that God will save Israel "if they do not continue in unbelief."[308] Certainly they won't, as the Apostle explains, concludes, and confirms, especially in Chapter eleven of the same epistle, stating:

"I say then, has God cast away his peoples? Certainly not." (Verse 1)

"God has not cast away his people whom he foreknew." (Verse 2)

---

[306]-(Romans 9:3-5)

[307]-(Romans 11:26,27 and Isaiah 59:20,21)

[308]-(Romans 11:23)

175

"I say then, have they stumbled that they should fall? Certainly not." (Verse 11)

"Now if their fall is riches for the world, and their failure riches for the Gentiles, how much more their fullness!" (Verse 12)

"For if their being cast away is the reconciling of the world, what will their acceptance be but life from the dead?" (Verse 15)

Then, addressing the Romans, he says:

"For I do not desire, brethren, that you shall be ignorant of this mystery, lest you should be wise in your own opinion, that <u>hardening</u> in <u>part</u> has happened to Israel until the fullness of the Gentiles has come in." (Verse 25)

"And so all Israel will be saved." (Verse 26)

For "concerning the election, they are beloved for the sake of the Fathers. For the gifts and the calling of God are irrevocable." (Verses 28, 29)

Thus, although gradually, salvation of "all Israel" in the past as in the coming future, is definite, absolute, inevitable, and irrevocable. For:

Many Israelites were saved by Jesus himself at his first coming, and by his disciples and apostles thereafter, as it is clearly and fully

176

related in the four Gospels, the Book of Acts, and in the Epistles of the Apostles.

Many others by the preachers and teachers of the Gospel through the whole course of Christendom history until the present time.

And finally, and before the Second Coming of Christ the Son of Man, the last remnant of Israel will be saved, in turn, by His grace and compassion according to Scriptures.

This is another of Pauline master mysteries that the Apostle of the Gentiles want us, we, Christian of all times, not to ignore; and by it he also warns us not to "boast" (of being Christian) "but (rather) fear"; for the gracious and righteous God, may cast us in turn, if we continue in unbelief, unrighteousness, and haughtiness.[309]

-3-

From the beginning, Jesus Christ did not come as a great monarch, or King of Kings, to rule a people, or a nation, or the whole world. For, from the beginning to the end his Kingdom "is an everlasting Kingdom."[310]

---

[309]-(Romans 11:18-24)

[310]-(Daniel 4:3 and Luke 1:33)

177

And though being the utmost rich, powerful,[311] and righteous God,[312] Christ lived poorly:

He was born "wrapped in swaddling clothes, and lying in a (mean) manger."[313] Up to the age of thirty, he lived as a common carpenter;[314] "having never studied."[315] Even during the three years of his ministry on earth, he was almost needy,[316] homeless,[317] spending often all his nights on a mountain praying.[318] And though being a heavenly King,[319] he entered Jerusalem "sitting on a donkey's colt."[320] And he said to Pilate, "My Kingdom is not of

---

[311]-*(Revelation 1:33)*

[312]-*(Psalm 7:9 and 11:7 and 2 Timothy 4:8 and 1 John 2:1)*

[313]-*(Luke 2:7)*

[314]-*(Mark 6:3)*

[315]-*(John 7:15)*

[316]-*(Matthew 17:27 and Luke 8:2,3)*

[317]-*(Matthew 8:20 and Luke 9:58)*

[318]-*(Luke 6:12 and 21:37)*

[319]-*(Luke 23:1-4)*

[320]-*(John 12:15 and Ezekiel 9:9)*

this world."[321] Moreover, the wisemen from the East came to Jerusalem and asked, "Where is he who has been King of the Jews?"[322] yet, "his own did not receive him."[323]

Thus, throughout his lifetime on earth Christ was enduring the sufferings of the cross, even before bearing his heavy cross on the way to Golgotha. Wherefore he was urging his disciples to bear their cross if they want to be worthy of him.[324]

Thus, Jesus Christ who is called King by God himself (Psalm 2:6), has been, however, rejected, rather denied by his own people (John 10:15 and 19:21).

Since his first coming, Jesus Christ could have established a worldly Kingdom. But he refused to do so.[325] He rejected such "Kingdoms of the world and their glory."[326] He could have

---

[321]-(John 18:26)

[322]-(Matthew 2:1-2)

[323]-(John 1:11)

[324]-(Matthew 16:24 and Mark 8:34 and Luke 9:23)

[325]-(John 6:15)

[326]-(Matthew 4:9 and Luke 5:8)

ordered his angels to defend him, either by his proper power, or by prayer to his Father.[327]

No one has portrayed this anchoritic form of life of Christ on earth, like St. Ephrem who says:

"Jesus died to the world in order that no one should live to the world, and He existed in a crucified body, in order that no one should walk sensually by it."

"He died to our world in His body in order that He may make (us) alive by his body to His world."

"And he mortified the life of the body in order that we may not live carnally by flesh."

"He is made the Master, a teacher not in tribulation of others but by his own sufferings."

"And He himself first tasted bitterness and (thereby) He showed us that no one can become His disciple by name but through suffering."[328]

---

[327]-*(Matthew 26:53)*

[328]-*History of Asceticism in the Syrian Orient II Early Monasticism in Mesopotamia and Syria. By Arthur Voobus, Dr. Theol. (Tarto) Lovain. Secretariat Du Corpusco. 49 Ch. De Wavre 1960. Page 98.*

So, if from the outset, Jesus Christ did not come in great glory and spectacular splendor, why then expect him to come anew as King of Kings, or Lord of Lords, for a reign of one millennium? Simply to impose his will upon earth and all nations? or to display his ultimate and absolute power and pomp?

The response is: No. No, according to Scriptures themselves. Throughout all his ministry on earth, Jesus Christ, the "gentle and lowly in heart,"[329] and the true God and Son of God, who never ceased doing God's works and wonders,[330] did not boast or proclaim publicly, or loudly, his divinity, save on some occasions whenever the time was appropriate to declare it.[331]

Therefore, we certainly blunder if we wait again (like the nonbeliever in Christ at his first coming) for a second coming of the Son of Man, expecting the establishment on earth of a worldwide Kingdom for one thousand years and meanwhile, people will routinely eat and drink, marry and give in marriage "as in the days of

---

[329]-*(Matthew 11:29)*

[330]-*(John 5:17)*

[331]-*(Luke 11:20 and John 8:58 and 10:30 and 14:9 and so on)*

Noah before the flood,"[332] or as in our present days, and the like.

Moreover as attests the Orthodox Study Bible: "Though most did not, a few early Fathers and writers believed in a literal **thousand year** binding of Satan and reign of Christ and the saints on earth. The Church, however, authoritatively rejected this teaching (called *Chiliasm* at the Second Ecumenical Council).[333]

No, the second coming of Christ will certainly not be for the "inauguration of his millennial reign when for a thousand years he will rule without a rival, and with the final assize and the assignment of the Devil of all satanic forces, and the wicked dead to eternal perdition."[334] For, as the same "popular evangelical preacher, pastor, and author" (The cover of this book) does describe justly, properly, and very brilliantly the very Kingdom of Christ, when he states:

"In his teaching, Jesus is to be seen substituting for the <u>political</u> conception the idea

---

[332]-*(Matthew 24:37-38)*

[333]-*Orthodox Study Bible, p 627.*

[334]-*Everything Jesus Taught; by Herbert Lockyer. Harper & Row Publishers, San Francisco, copyright 1976,1984. Page 500.*

of the Kingdom which was spiritual in its nature, and by consequence, universal with its essentially spiritual character revealed in the nature of the blessings it brings."[335]

In this second statement of Herbert Lockyer about the spiritual Kingdom of Christ (from the outset), is he not contradicting himself (in his first one) when he thinks of a pure worldly Kingdom of Christ for one thousand years on earth? And thereby, is he not contradicting also the following statement of another great preacher of the Gospel who is Billy Graham when he, in turn, asserts that during "Christ's reign" on earth:

"Political confusion will be turned to order and harmony, social injustices will be abolished, and moral corruption will be replaced by integrity. For the first time in history the whole world will know what it is like to live in a society governed by God's principles. And Satan's influence will not be present to hinder world progress toward peace, unity, equality, and justice. Man's dream for global harmony will be realized!"[336]

In this statement, also, isn't the worldly Kingdom of men substituted for another

---

[335]-*Ibid. page 507.*

[336]-*Till Armageddon: A Perspective on Suffering. Copyright 1981. Pp. 22,23.*

worldly Kingdom of Christ? Besides, such a worldly Kingdom of one thousand years on earth "governed by God's principles" does remind us of Plato's Republic governed by Philosopher's principles. As a final result, both of them will remain worldly and not spiritual.

Neither in the past, nor in the near or distant future, the Kingdom of Christ was, or would be, universally terrestrial, or physical, by any means. Jesus himself confirmed to Pilate: "My Kingdom is not of this world...My Kingdom is not from here."[337] And the Apostle Paul ridicules in advance such a worldly Kingdom. He expresses this very clearly and categorically as well when he says to the Romans: "For the Kingdom of God is not food, and drink, but righteousness, and peace, and joy in the Holy Spirit."[338]

Besides, by setting a specific number of "one thousand years" for the reign of Christ on earth, which, up to this very moment, did not occur (and if it will occur sooner or later) are not, these preachers and teachers of the Gospel, anticipating, somehow, the Day of the Lord? Aren't they, unavoidably, postponing Christ's Second and Final Coming as well? And aren't they, also, indirectly or rather directly, fixing in advance, the date or the Day

---

[337]-(John 18:36)

[338]-(Romans 14:17)

of the Son of Man, that even the angels of heaven are unaware of?[339]

Furthermore, why then, replace (during the millennium era) the Holy Spirit, by the One who sent him,[340] i.e., Jesus Christ himself, who, with the Father and the Holy Spirit, is with us "always even to the end of age?"[341] Otherwise, was the Holy Spirit hitherto, as an interim, only for a while? Namely, till the "millennium" of these preachers and teachers of the Gospel?

-4-

Christ's peace has been established once and for all on earth and in the hearts of men. It has been established during his first coming as the prophet predicted:

"For unto us a child is born, unto us a Son is given; and the government will be under his shoulders. And his name will be called Wonderful, Counselor, Mighty God, Everlasting Father, Prince of Peace." Of the increase of his government and peace there will be no end."[342]

---

[339]-(Matthew 24:36 and Mark 13:32)

[340]-(John 15:26 and 16:7)

[341]-(Matthew 28:20)

[342]-(Isaiah 9:6,7)

185

"He shall speak peace to the nation."[343]

And as the Angels of heaven heralded praising and saying:

"Glory to God in the highest, and on earth peace, good will toward men."[344]

And as Christ himself prophesied and promised to leave his very peace with us, and to give it to us:

"Peace I have with you. My peace I give to you, not as the world gives do I give to you."[345]

And as the Apostle Paul, writing to the Philippians, said, "And the peace of God, which surpasses all understanding, will guard your hearts and minds through Christ Jesus.[346]

Therefore, Christ's peace is, by far, more genuine, more strong, and more durable than any other worldly peaces, and pacts, and treaties. It is this same and very peace of Christ that has changed the world. It replaced hostility with hospitality, hatred with friendship, brutality with benevolence and charity; crudeness and cruelty of pagans with refinement and gentleness of the Faithful. In and with Jesus only we have peace, true and everlasting peace.

---

[343]-*(Zechariah 9:10)*

[344]-*(Luke 2:13:14)*

[345]-*(John 14:27)*

[346]-*(Philippians 4:7)*

Whereas in the world, we have tribulations, worries, and wars.

Besides, despite wars, revolutions, struggles, and rivalries for expansion, dominion, and colonization (because also of greediness, despotism and madness of some Christian dictators or governments), "Christian civilization is probably the best that has been produced so far in human history."[347]

And Christ's peace, is indeed the true and peerless peace of meek men,[348] well defined in these beautiful terms: "the perfectly ordered and harmonious communion of those who find their joy in God, and in one another in God."[349]

No, No power on earth, or glory, or wealth, or any worldly government or institution can procure such a peace of Christ that Paul portrays so marvelously when he says to the Ephesians:

"For he himself is our peace, who has made both one, and has broken down the middle wall of division between us, having

---

[347]-*The Christ of the Indian Road. By E. Stanly Jones. The Abingdon Press, N.Y. Copyright 1925. Chapter 2, page 32.*

[348]-*(Matthew 5:5)*

[349]-*The City of God, By St. Augustine. Image Books Edition 1958. (The Introduction, page 10)*

abolished in his flesh the enmity, that is, the law of Commandments contained in ordinances, so as to create in Himself one new man from the two, thus making peace, and that He might reconcile them both to God in one body through the cross, thereby putting to death the enmity. And He came and preached peace to you who were afar off and to those who were near. For through Him we both have access by one spirit to the Father."[350]

Thus, it is absolutely wrong and deceiving as well, to say that "God promised to send His Son at the appointed time to reign over the earth and to begin His absolute rule of peace and justice. And so it will be that the rulers and their armies who resist Christ's return will be killed in mass carnage."[351] For Christ never in the past, killed, nor in the future, will kill people "in mass carnage." For Christ is always Prince of Peace. Therefore, no peace on earth, (in the past as in the future) settled by a universal treaty of Nations, or promulgated by the so-called Nation Security Council, match, or transcend the peace of those Christians, who, through the whole course of history, suffered harassment and humiliation until martyrdom from boorish hooligans and

---

[350]-*(Ephesians 2:14-14:18)*

[351]- *Armageddon, Oil and the Middle East Crisis. By John F. Walvooro Zondervan Publishing House. Grand Rapids, Michigan. Copyright 1974, 1976, 1990. Page 195.*

barbarous pagans of all sorts. Yes, it is of such a peace that creates an inner happiness that "no one", as Jesus consoled his followers, "will take your joy from you."[352] Yes, it is this same inner joy and peace that prompted Paul to assert exultantly in Christ: "For I am persuaded that neither death, nor life, nor angels, nor principalities, nor powers, nor things present, nor things to come, nor height, nor depths, nor any other created thing, shall be able to separate us from the love of God which is in Christ Jesus our Lord."[353]

For finally the true Kingdom of God is first and foremost "within us."[354] And our everlasting life after death is in heaven with Christ till eternity. Because only there, and not in this world, that God "will wipe away every tear from the eyes of every believer in him, especially from the eyes of his saints and martyrs. As only there, in heaven, "shall be no more death, nor sorrow, nor crying; and there shall be no more pain, for the former things have passed away."[355]

---

[352]-*(John 16:22)*

[353]-*(Romans 8:38)*

[354]-*(Luke 17:21)*

[355]-*(Revelation 21:41)*

189

Therefore, there is peace on earth, when there is peace in the hearts. And there is peace in our hearts: When "evil things" are cast out of our hearts,[356] and when "desires for pleasure that war in" our members are chased out in turn.[357] At that very moment only:

Christ himself will indwell our hearts "through faith."[358] As peace of God "will rule our hearts,"[359] not only for one thousand years,[360] but for ever and evermore.

---

[356]-*(Matthew 18:19)*

[357]-*(James 4:1)*

[358]-*(Ephesians 3:17)*

[359]-*(Colossians 3:15)*

[360]-*(Revelations 20:4)*

III

A HIGH WAY FOR AN EASY CHRISTIANITY

-1-

An easy Christianity, is a Christianity without Christ; Christ without a cross, crucifixion, and resurrection.

An easy Christianity, is a Bible without a Law; a law without commandments to revere and keep forever.

An easy Christianity, is a Church without an altar; an altar without "an offering and sacrifice to God for a sweet-smelling aroma."[359]

Thus, an easy Christianity, is a pagan cult, called also the very "wide gate and broad way that leads to destruction, and there are many who go in by it." [360] For it is the way of limitless liberty and libertinism as well; of

---

[359]-*(Ephesians 5:2)*

[360]-*(Matthew 7:13)*

193

worldly wealth and success; of a mere merriment, selfishness, and self-esteem.

As many are also pseudo-preachers of the gospel who teach such a loose, and easy Christianity based exclusively on an abstract and aberrant faith alone in Christ. Because, here too, it is easier to neglect or reject Christ's commandments than to keep them; to do evil than to practice righteousness; to free our instincts themselves, than to emancipate ourselves from lusts and lecheries of the world; to live, in brief, indecently, than "to discipline (our) body, and bring it into subjection."[361]

Christianity, real Christianity, genuine Christianity, is not a common or current religion as all other religions of the world. It is rather Christ himself who declared emphatically, "I am the Way, the Truth, and the Life"[362] and, "I am the door. If anyone enters by me, he will be saved."[363]

Therefore, the entrance or the entry to heaven is through Christ alone who is "the

---

[361]-(1 Corinthians 9:27)

[362]-(John 14:6)

[363]-(John 10:9)

door", or the "narrow gate;" the "way, or difficult way" "which leads to life, and there are few who find it."[364] And as attests emphatically the Apostle Peter, "Nor is there salvation in any other, for there is no other name under heaven given among men by which we must be saved."[365]

However, yes, this good and godly door, or gate, or way to heaven, is <u>narrow</u> and <u>difficult</u>.

It is "narrow", because to pass through, we have to follow Christ alone, bear his Cross, keep his commandments, and reject therefore the "works of the flesh" that Paul sums up in the following: "Adultery, fornication, uncleanness, licentiousness, idolatry, sorcery, hatred, contentions, jealousies, outbursts of wrath, selfish ambitions, dissensions, heresies, envy, murders, drunkenness, revelries, and the like; of which I tell you beforehand, just as I also told you in time past, that those who

---

[364]-*(Matthew 7:13,14)*

[365]-*(Acts 4:12)*

practice such things will not inherit the Kingdom of God."[366]

And it is "difficult," because to follow Christ is also to endure persecution.[367] For here too, it suffices to be a disciple of Christ or "the light of the world"[368] so that "every one practicing evil, hates the light."[369] Saint Paul writes also to Timothy, "yes, and all who desire to live a godly life in Christ Jesus will suffer persecution."[370]

Therefore, very few are those who find Christ and follow him faithfully, trustfully, and wholeheartedly.

Now, how come that Christ, after comparing himself to a narrow gate and difficult way which leads to life, says, on the

---

[366]-(Galatians 5:19-21 and Romans 1:29-32 and 1 Corinthians 6:9,10)

[367]-"Matthew 5:10)

[368]-(Matthew 5:14)

[369]-(John 3:20)

[370]-(2 Timothy 3:12)

other hand, that his "Yoke is easy and (his) burden is light?"[371]

Being based on love, faith, hope, grace, forgiveness, plus "great reward in heaven,"[372] Christ's yoke is "easy" indeed, and his "burden," undeniably light and lovely, only to those who truly love him, and keep gladly and heartily his commandments. Paul says exultantly, "For I am persuaded that neither death, nor life, nor angels, nor principalities, nor powers, nor things present, nor things to come, nor height, nor depth, nor any other created thing, shall be able to separate us from the love of God which is in Christ Jesus our Lord."[373]

-2-

"On the face of it, it would be hard to imagine a nation thoroughly biblical than the United States between the American Revolution and the Civil War."[374]

---

[371]-*(Matthew 12:30)*

[372]-*(Matthew 4:12 and Luke 6:23)*

[373]-*(Romans 9:38,39)*

[374]-*The Bible in America. Edited by Nathan O. Hatch and Mark A. Noll. Oxford University Press, Inc. Copyright 1982. Page 39.*

No, never ever, America has stopped or ceased to be a religious and a biblical nation, albeit somehow infuriating Christ with an apparent, persistent and pervasive immorality.

For, "In God we trust" says still "Scripture" on America's money, although materialistic America, seems, nowadays, to trust much more Mammon than God.

"One Nation under God" is America's motto. And America's God is Christ Jesus. But, secular America alone is no more under God Christ. But isn't America as a whole, a Christian state? Wasn't it found from the outset by Christian Fathers and Founders? Who then prohibits Christian America from adoring, worshiping and praying Christ God in her proper schools and universities?

For while Solomon urges all generations saying, "Remember now your Creator in the days of your youth,"[375] it is only liberal America that prohibits her youth from lifting up prayer to God Christ, the very God of Christian America, even in their own schools and universities. Aren't Catholics, Jews and Muslims for instance in America teaching their children their own religions in their private schools?

---

[375]-*(Ecclesiastes 12:1)*

What then again prevents, precludes and prohibits Christian Protestants in their America from doing so in her own public schools and universities? Otherwise, i.e. if public schools are for minorities, shut their public schools. Period. But if the overwhelming majority of students in public schools are Christians of different denominations, why over again, deprive them from their self-evident right to be taught Christian ethics? Why not, hence, amend the First Amendment? Isn't Son of Man Lord of the Sabbath?[376] and Lord of the Constitution as well?

"I pledge allegiance to the flag of the United States of America" declare American citizens at public meetings, standing up and placing their right hands over their hearts. Whereas nominal Americans, dare burn deliberately and publicly the same flag they pledged allegiance to (and no one budges, blames, and punishes the traitors).

Nevertheless, despite this great and unprecedented movement of preaching and teaching the word of God in America, the insidious seepage and spread of immorality (that stem particularly from Capitals, Metropolises and big cities) seem to bedevil the

---

[376]-*(Matthew 12:8)*

body of the entire Nation, as all studies and surveys daily show. Among these infectious immoralities, for instance: Alcoholism, drug addiction, pornography, homosexuality, thuggery, raping, abortion, divorce, adultery, fornication, smuggling, love of money, disrespect of parents, superiority complex, violence and violation of both the Law of God and the law of State (And that is because of limitless liberty that stifles and suppresses liberty itself, guaranteed or granted by the First Amendment) - No wonder the familiar curse "I hate you" has become in America, somehow, the common and current slogan of a new perverse generation, that lacks the basic human foundation that is Character. (As defined by the American Heritage Dictionary, Character is "The combined moral ethical structure of a person or group" or "Moral or ethical strength, integrity, fortitude."

Addressing "the 1,385 graduates of Dartmouth College yesterday at the 221st commencement ceremony held on the campus in Hanover, N.H."; Elizabeth Dole, American Red Cross president said, "It is your moral compass that counts far more than any bank balance, any resume and, yes, any diploma", she said. "Whether on the floor of congress or in the board-rooms of corporate America or in the corridors of a big city hospital, there is no body of professional expertise and no anthology of care studies which can supplant the force of character which provides both a sense of direction and means of fulfillment. It asks, not what you want to be, but who you want to be."[377]

And the other perilous plague and disastrous disease of all ages, is Aids. Because, here too, as the Apostle Paul says, "Men did commit what is shameful" and did receive thereby "in themselves" (as in others) the penalty of their error which was due."[378]

Concerning permissiveness in America (and in the other so called civilized nations), some may mock you if you label them licentious or immoral. Nudity and flaunting of the flesh are on display in movies, televisions, stages, beaches, casinos, clubs, hotels, circles, subways, buses, streets, parks, shopping centers, offices; nay, magazines, newspapers, commercials and even in schools, homes, temples and churches themselves on many occasions.

---

[377]-*The New York Times National. Monday, June 10, 1991.*

[378]-*(Romans 1:27)*

Now, if the simple act of "looking at a woman to lust for her" is already considered as "adultery with her in (one's) heart,"[379] how much more covetous the human eye would be if women are dressed provocatively and so indecently; or dancing totally nude in some movies and clubs!

Isn't it because women, in the ancient Roman pagan world, were also indecently dressed up, that the Apostle Paul expressed his desire that Christian women should "adorn themselves in modest apparel, with propriety and moderation?"[380]

Besides his two wives Ahinoam the Jezreelitess and Abigail the widow of Nabal the Carmelite[381] and his many "concubines and wives" he took thereafter,[382] David saw the "very beautiful Bathsheba bathing" and lusted after her nakedness. The great prophet, coveted and lusted after her. And as a powerful king, he also killed Uriah, her husband (a chief commander of his own army), and took her as a

---

[379]-(Matthew 5:28)

[380]-(1 Timothy 2:8,9)

[381]-(2 Samuel 2:2)

[382]-(2 Samuel 5:13)

wife?[383] But this strange event happened in the distant past before the coming of Christ into the world. Whereas, nowadays, and, somehow adultery, fornication, rape, divorce, crimes, thefts, abortions and the like are taking place in Christian continents. Permissive nudity and flaunting of the flesh are so cheaply and shamelessly displayed. Didn't the Scriptures themselves state, "And they knew that they were naked, and they sewed the leaves together and made themselves a covering. . . and hid themselves from the presence of the Lord God among the trees of the garden?"[384] Moreover, isn't God Himself, who, according to Moses, "made tunics of skin and clothed them"[385] namely, Adam and Eve?

No, I don't like to exaggerate and say like Leartes to Ophelia his sister (In Shakespeare's "Hamlet the Prince of Denmark, Act I, Scene III),

> "The chariest maid is prodigal enough If she unmask her beauty to the moon."

---

[383]-(2 Samuel 11:2-18)

[384]-(Genesis 7:3,8)

[385]-(Genesis 3:21)

But isn't it too much, this exorbitance and extravagance of fleshy displays and sauntering of women naked in the so-called civilized Christian world? Do genuine Christian families permit or admit heartily, or wholeheartedly, that their mothers, or wives, or daughters, or sisters exhibit publicly such a noxious nudism?

Reports the New York Times, Saturday, June 22, 1991 on his first and front page, "Washington, June 21 -The Supreme Court ruled today that while nude dancing is a form of expression entitled to a measure of First Amendment protection, states may ban it in the interest of "protecting order and morality." The 5-to-4 decision upheld a public indecency law in Indiana as applied to nude performances in a night club and adult bookstore in South Bend. The law, similar to laws in effect in some two dozen other states, required female performers to wear at least panties and a G-string."

And the simple question in this respect, is: Where is the "slightest" difference between "nude dancing" and dancing with "panties and a G-string"? There is rather a notable twist, a flaw in the spirit of the law itself. Is it in such a shameful way or "rule" that the Supreme Court, according to the First Amendment, "protect order and morality" in America?

And the second crucial, rather primordial question: Do American preachers and teachers of the gospel, particularly, attack, or react, or inveigh against such pernicious permissiveness? Do they urge, in their churches, sermons, and publications, the American women to adorn themselves "with propriety and moderation" as the Apostle Paul did two thousand years ago? Or are they, rather, modernizing Christianity according to the New Age, and for the sole purpose, of pleasing here, a new perverse generation?

About "America's Future" writes Anthony Lewis, "Every year, 1 million teenager girls almost a tenth of the age group, become pregnant; 2.5 million adolescents contract a sexually transmitted disease."[386]

And, what report almost daily all polls, surveys, studies and statistics about this flagrant and fatal immorality in America, is indeed more catastrophic and calamitous. They report for instance:

That more than 50 percent of youths are getting sexual relations even before the age of 18.

---

[386]-*The New York Times, Friday, July 6, 1990.*

That more than 75 percent of all males and females have sex before marriage.

That each year more than one million babies are conceived out of wedlock.

That more than half a million illegitimate births does occur every year.

That more than one million couples divorce each year (i.e., 2 out of 3).

That more than 56 percent of husbands and wives commit adultery even before the age of 40.

That more than 20 million are regular users of marijuana; and more than 10 million are cocaine abusers, and more than a half million heroin addicts.

That sales of narcotics total more than $100 billion annually.

And so on, and so forth.

Now, for another instance, if the American preachers and teachers of the Gospel, were really tough enough in divorce, they should explain and warn that "whoever divorces his wife (or her husband) for any reason, except sexual immorality, causes her (or him) to commit adultery,"[387] meaning that both of them are considered as sinners, and deserve, in consequence, damnation. Of course, because of the abuse and misuse of marriage's relationship, insanity of either partner, and the like, the Church, according to Christ's authorization: "Whatever you bind on earth will be bound in heaven, and whatever you loose on earth will be loosed in heaven,"[388] gave a dispensation for divorce.

And if the American preachers and teachers of the Gospel were zealously and strenuously teaching people, they should advise them:

To respect marriage, which St. Paul calls "great mystery" in Ephesians 5:32. For, what is this "great mystery," marvels St. John Chrysostom, so that a girl, in one single day, begins to feel affection for a man she didn't see before, and to love him as she loves her own body? (namely to accept to be his wife) And "what is this "great mystery;" that a man, in one single day, falls in love with a girl he didn't know or meet before, and to prefer her to all his friends, relatives and even his own

---

[387]-*(Matthew 5:32 and Mark 10:11,12)*

[388]-*(Matt. 18:18)*

parents?[389] (Namely to prefer her to be her husband).

"That what God has joined together, let no man separate,"[390] neither any institution.

To love their wives "as their own bodies,"[391] as Christ also "loved the church and gave himself for it."[392]

Yes again, if the American preachers and teachers of the Gospel were constantly exhorting and teaching their congregants, to respect marriage and refrain from divorce, certainly marriage wouldn't be so insecure and vulnerable in America, and divorce so loose and so in vogue; and family (the backbone of every great nation) so threatened and humbled, in consequence.

---

[389]-*On Priesthood. Conversations about Marriage. Letters to Olympia. Translated to Arabic by Archbishop Stephanos Haddad. Publication of AL-NUR. Copyright 1982-Beirut, Lebanon (The Selection of a Wife. Page 174).*

[390]-*(Matthew 19:6 and Mark 10:9)*

[391]-*(Ephesians 5:28)*

[392]-*(Ephesians 5:25)*

Asked once, if "whoever marries her (or him) who is divorced except of sexual immorality does he (or she) commit adultery?"[393] a classical teacher of the Bible on radio answered, "Yes indeed; but if they repent, their sin, by Christ's blood, is washed away and forgiven." This same preacher and teacher of the Gospel gave the same answer to a remarried woman (who committed thereby adultery twice). Another noted Televangelist (for around a quarter of a century) stated that a married man with two children left his wife and fell in love with his secretary and married her. Then He asked, "Do you call her a whore? (namely the man's secretary) Didn't Paul himself say, "For the good that I will to do, I do not do; but the evil I will not to do, that I practice etc."?[394] And departing thus from this statement of Paul, our noted Evangelist preached forgiveness for both of them, the man with two children who divorced his legitimate wife, and his secretary whom he married against the law and the Scriptures themselves.

No, never ever the sin of the above mentioned remarried men and women are forgiven or washed away by Christ's blood.

---

[393]-(Matthew 19:9 and Mark 10:12 and Luke 16:18)

[394]-(Romans 7:19,20)

Otherwise they can get remarried or redivorced scores of times and be forgiven! For Christ's blood does cleanse and wash only sins of those who repent sincerely and stop sinning; those who really love Christ and keep his commandments.[395] Those redivorced or remarried men and women will never ever inherit the kingdom of heaven for they are still sinners,[396] until and unless they stop definitely their sinful relationships, and repent and return to their legitimate husbands and wives if they are still alive.[397] Or again as says Paul, "Are you bound to a wife? (i.e. are you married?) Do not seek to be loosed. (i.e. divorced). Are you loosed from a wife? Do not seek a wife. But even if you do marry, (i.e. as a single) you have not sinned.[398]

Being in such a sinful state, Claudius (in Shakespeare's "Hamlet of Denmark") who murdered his own brother (the real King), married his wife, and usurped his throne, says rightly and rigorously while praying,

---

[395]-*(John 14:15)*

[396]-*(1 Corinthians 6:9)*

[397]-*(1 Corinthians 7:39)*

[398]-*(1 Corinthians 7:27.28)*

". . .Pray can I not. . .
That cannot be, since I still possessed
of these effects for which I did the
murder,
My crown, mine own ambition, and my
queen."
(Acts 3, Scene 4)

Although arguably not a notorious
believer, Shakespeare is interpreting here the
very right statement of the Gospel itself, and
echoing thereby the genuine belief of the
Church and the holy tradition of sixteen
centuries of Christendom.

-3-

Whereas Christ says, "Therefore you
shall be perfect just as your Father in heaven is
perfect"[399] and, "For I say to you, that unless
your righteousness exceeds the righteousness of
the scribes and Pharisees, you by no means
enter the kingdom of heaven,"[400] the astonishing
thing is to see even Martin Luther himself
declaring somehow in a very tolerant way,
"When the Devil tempts us with annoying
persistency, it may be wise to yield him a sin or

---

[399]-*(Matthew 5:48)*

[400]-*(Matthew 5:20)*

two; Seek out the society of your boon companions, drink, play, talk loudly, and amuse yourself. <u>One</u> <u>must</u> <u>sometimes</u> <u>commit</u> <u>sin</u> out of hate and contempt for the Devil, so as not to give him the chance to make one scrupulous over mere nothing; if one is too frightened of sinning, one is lost. . . Oh if I could find some really good sin that would give the Devil a toss."[401]

Although to Luther himself, the finding of a "good sin" is impossible, his statement as a whole seems too daring. For neither David who cautioned not to stand "in the path of sinners,[402] nor Paul who exhorted Timothy to "flee youthful lusts and pursue righteousness"[403] did dare declare such a libertine claim or call, to such a hint of permissiveness "For the wages of sin (all sorts of sins) is death."[404]

As if he is addressing Luther's stand toward sin, "Good sin or great sin altogether,"

---

[401]-*The Story of Civilization. By Will Durant. Simon and Schuster. N.Y. 1957 (Caesar and Christ. The Reformation in Germany. Luther's Theology. Page 374).*

[402]-*(Psalm 1:1)*

[403]-*(2 Timothy 2:22)*

[404]-*(Romans 6:32)*

Spurgeon says very rightly, "If you once mount into sin, there is no stopping. Take heed, if you would not become the worst of characters, take heed of the little sins, which, mounting one upon another, may at last heave you from the summit and destroy your soul forever. There is a great danger in secret sins. . Let us take heed of our little sins. A little sin, like a little pebble in the shoe, will make a traveler to heaven walk very wearily. . . Little sins, like little thieves, may open the door to greater ones outside. . . Little sins, like little stains in silk, may damage the fine texture of fellowship. Little sins, like little irregulations in the machinery, may spoil the whole of your religion."[405]

When the Apostle Paul advises the Corinthians saying, "But this I say, brethren, the time is short (meaning our lifetime or age is short in the world, and not as Will Durante pretends saying: "The Apostles were apparently unanimous in believing that Christ would soon return to establish the Kingdom of heaven on earth.")[406] so that from now on even those who have wives should be as though they had none,"

---

[405]-*Spurgeon's Sermons. Volume 3. Baker Book House. Grand Rapids, Michigan. Copyright 1985. Page 174.*

[406]-*The story of civilization, V III, Caesar and Christ, Simeon and Schuster, New York, copyright 1944, page 575).*

(meaning that although marriage is holy, married people should love Christ more than each other[407] (in a sense, not to be so attached to the worldly pleasures so that to carry one's self with total indifference even to the love of our Creator who is our final and ultimate goal). And Paul continues, "those who weep as though they did not weep, those who rejoice as though they did not rejoice, those who buy as though they did not possess, and those who use this world as not using it. For the form of this world is passing away."[408]

Matthew Henry comments on these statements of Paul and infers very fairly saying, "General rules to all Christians to carry themselves with a holy indifference towards the world. . . We must keep the world out of our hearts, that we may not abuse it when we have it in our hands. We have but little time to continue in this world. Therefore do not set your hearts on worldly enjoyments. Do not be overwhelmed with worldly cares and troubles. It is not so much a world as the appearance of one. All is shown with nothing solid in its and it

---

[407]-*(Matthew 10:37)*

[408]-*(1 Corinthians 7:29-31)*

214

is transient show too, and will quickly be gone".
(V.31)[409]

Thus, as Christians, our final abode is in heaven with Christ. Therefore we have to love Christ more than the world and all the things of the world. And to love Christ, we have to keep his commandments, and endeavor to emulate him and be as perfect as he himself is.

Therefore, in like manner of Solomon's saying, "Do not be overly righteous,"[410] and the Hellenistic's "happy medium," Luther's advice, "One must sometimes commit sin" etc. etc. and the like, are not very Christian. Christianity is against "medium standing or stance"; "I know your work, that you are neither cold nor hot, I could wish you were cold or hot. So then, because you are lukewarm, and neither cold nor hot, I will spew you out of my mouth."[411]

Again, this so-called "in between" or "in between stand on the issue," doesn't exist in the gospel. Either you are with Christ or with the

---

[409]-*Matthew Henry's Commentary on the Whole Bible. Copyright 1961 by Zondervan Publishing House. Grand Rapids, Michigan.*

[410]-*(Ecclesiastes 7:16)*

[411]-*(Revelation 3:15,16)*

215

world; with God or with mammon, a "branch" in Christ or cast out of Christ and withered.[412] As Paul put it in his marvelous way: "Do not be unequally yoked together with unbelievers. For what fellowship has righteousness with lawlessness? And what communion has light with darkness? And what accord has Christ with Belial? Or what part has a believer with an unbeliever? And what agreement has the temple of God with idols? For you are the temple of the living God."[413] "Therefore, having these promises, beloved, let us cleanse ourselves from all filthiness of the flesh and spirit, perfecting holiness in the fear of God."[414]

In "The Character of Methodist" the British Founder of Methodism, John Wesley says: "For as he (the Methodist) loves God, so he keeps his commandments, not only some or most of them, but all, from the least to the greatest. He is not content to "Keep the whole law and offend in one point," but has in all points "a conscience void of offense toward God and toward men" whatever God has forbidden, he avoids, whatever God hath

---

[412]-*(John 10:5,6)*

[413]-*(2 Corinthians 6:14-16)*

[414]-*(2 Corinthians 7:1)*

enjoined, he doeth; and that whatever it be little or great, hard or easy, joyous or grievous to the flesh. He "runs the way of God's commandments", now he hath set his heart at liberty. . . All the commandments of God he accordingly keeps, did that with all his might."[415]

-4-

Salvation by Jesus Christ, was planned and prepared even "before the time began," and before any good works or deeds on the part of men themselves. In that respect the Apostle Paul says, "Therefore do not be ashamed of the testimony of our Lord, nor of me his prisoner, but share with me in the sufferings for the gospel according to the power of God, who has saved us and called us with a holy calling not according to our works, but according to his own purpose and grace which was given to us in Christ Jesus before the time began, but has now been revealed by the appearing of our Savior Jesus Christ, who has abolished death and brought life and immortality to light through

---

[415]-*Great Voices of the Reformation. By Harry Emerson Fosdick. A Modern Library Giant. New York. Copyright 1952. John Wesley. Page 510.*

the gospel to which I was appointed a preacher, an apostle, and teacher of the Gentiles."[416]

And as the Apostle Peter states that we "were not redeemed with corruptible things, like silver or gold, from (our) aimless conduct received by tradition from (our) fathers, but with the precious blood of Christ, as of a lamb without blemish and without spot. He indeed was foreordained before the foundation of the world; but was manifested in these last times for (us)."[417]

This means, that even before any preceding, or preparatory kind of good works and deeds on our part, "while we were still sinners, Christ died for us."[418]

Thus, God himself, did plan to save us, even "before the time began" or "before the foundation of the world;" without any preceding works on our part. Excluding not however, (in the pseudo-pretext and plea of being saved beforehand by the "precious blood of Christ" or "by grace" and gratis) the practice of any further

---

[416]-(2 Timothy 1:8-12)

[417]-(1 Peter 1:18-20)

[418]-(Romans 5:8)

good deeds and works on our part. For, of such an attempt or intention, the Apostle Peter reminds us, "as he who called you is holy you also be holy in all your conduct, because it is written, "Be holy, for I am holy." And if you call on the Father, who without partiality judges according to each one's work, conduct yourselves throughout the time of your rejoining here in fear."[419]

In this regard, saint John Chrysostom says: ". . .since then it has given us life, let us remain living and not return again to the former deadness: for 'Christ dies no more; for the death that He died, He died unto sin once'[420] and He will not have us always saved by grace, for so we will be empty of all things. Therefore, He will have us contribute something from ourselves as well. Let us then contribute, and preserve life for our soul."[421]

In their explanation of the doctrine of salvation, both Paul and Peter put the stress and emphasis on salvation by "grace," "faith,"

---

[419]-(1 Peter 1:15-17)

[420]-(Rom. 6:9-10)

[421]-(John Chrysostom, homily 6 on 2 Cor. 3:2-3, from the Bible and the holy Fathers for Orthodox, Monastery books, Menlo Park CA, 1990, page 295)

"the precious blood of Christ," and "the gift of God;" and not at all because of any precedent or antecedent good works of ourselves. Therefore the apostle Paul writes to the Ephesians saying, "For by grace you have been saved through faith, and that not of yourselves, it is the gift of God, not of works lest anyone should boast. For we are his workmanship created in Christ Jesus for good works, which God prepared beforehand that we should walk in them."[422]

Saint Paul means here, and especially here, that even though we have been saved "before the world began" and "before the foundation of the world" through God's grace and by faith in Christ, (and not because of good works on our part,) yet, as "workmanship, created in Christ Jesus for good works...we should walk in them. But by doing so, we should not brag and boast, but rather say always, "we are unprofitable servants. We have done what was duty to us."[423] Immanuel Kant put it this way, "It suffices not to do our duty, we should do it as a duty" or, "You should, then you can" expressing here too exactly what again the Apostle Paul said, "No temptation has

---

[422]-(Ephesians 2:8,9)

[423]-(Luke 17:10)

220

overtaken you except such as is common to man; but God is faithful, <u>who</u> <u>will</u> <u>not</u> <u>allow</u> <u>you</u> <u>to</u> <u>be</u> <u>tempted</u> <u>beyond</u> <u>what</u> <u>you</u> <u>are</u> <u>able</u>, but with the temptation will also make the way of escape, that you may be able to bear it".[424]

Contrary to most of the American preachers and teachers of the false equation:

FAITH + NOTHING[425] = SALVATION

Even a non-believer like Will Durant believes and asserts saying,"As to good works, combined with faith, Paul never <u>tired</u> of inculcating them; and the most famous words even spoken about love are his own."[426]

-5-

Therefore, I can't help but ask here: Doesn't a modernized media of preaching and teaching the gospel in America, become somehow, a very profitable, comfortable, suitable, and sweatless job as well? Isn't, in other terms, the video preacher very well

---

[424]-*(1 Corinthians 10:13)*

[425]-*(namely faith without work)*

[426]-*Ibid, page 589.*

sheltered, safe, and secure behind his TV screen and microphone, so that, unlike all apostles of old, he is no more exposed to the hatred and harassment of pagans and barbarians; not faced with their direct slanders, revilement, persecution, torment, torture and even to death by stoning or sword or crucifixion or the like?

Oh, how would I like to see this modern and video preacher and teacher of the Gospel, leaving from time to time his own folk and followers; and like Christ and his apostles and disciples, traveling, venturing, entering cities and synagogues, mingling with menacing masses, mobs and preaching the Jews and the Gentiles, the Moslems and the Buddhists, the secular and the heathen, and all sorts of sinners. For "those who are well have no need of physician, but those who are sick."[427]

For Christ is his teachings and his epistle written "by the Spirit of the Living God, not on tablets of stone, but on tablets of flesh, that is, of the heart."[428]

---

[427]-(Matthew 9:12 and Mark 2:17 and Luke 5:31)

[428]-(2 Corinthians 3:3)

But even, Christ's Sermon on the Mount, the greatest Manifesto of all times, if taken apart, or isolated; and if broadcasted or telecasted; and if published, or told publicly almost daily, it would certainly not impact people, unless and until it's embedded in the preacher's heart, mind and soul so that he can urge people to rightly and rigorously, "imitate (him) just as Paul himself also imitated Christ."[429]

Therefore, Christ's Sermon on the Mount should be manifested through the direct contact of the preacher with his parishioners, as through their mutual faithfulness and good behavior, so that when people see his and their good works, will glorify their Father in heaven.[430]

Furthermore, doesn't such a modern preaching of the Gospel alter and somehow hinder Christ's doctrine of salvation? Because if it does not truly lead to the closing of local churches, it would at least prohibit the faithful from gathering together "with one accord in

---

[429]-(1 Corinthians 11:1)

[430]-(Matthew 5:16 and 2 Peter 2:12)

223

one place;"[431] "breaking bread,"[432] and partaking "of that one bread,"[433] and praying and praising God. "For where two or three are gathered together in my name, says Jesus, I am there in the midst of them."[434]

The evangelist Jerry Falwell says, as reported by the New York Times National Sunday, March 3, 1991, "I see local churches where gospel is preached and needs are met on a personal basis, as the future of this country."

-6-

Says Herbert Lockyer, "There is no salvation through the life, He (Christ) lived among men, even although there are those who teach salvation by imitation: Live like Jesus, imbibe His teachings, emulate His example, and all will be right. But Christ after the flesh is not

---

[431]-*(Acts 1:14 and 2:11 and 2:44 and 1 Corinthians 14:23)*

[432]-*(Acts 2:46)*

[433]-*(1 Corinthians 10:17)*

[434]-*(Matthew 18:20)*

224

a Savior,"[435] painting thereby the picture of a permissive, easy, and false Christianity that will definitely lead to destruction.

Obviously and erroneously enough, Herbert Lockyer wants to say, "Although Christ alone is the sole Holy who could keep the whole law of God (that is quite correct), there is, however, no salvation through his own righteousness. So don't try, therefore, to be as righteous as He is. Don't imitate him. Don't assimilate his teachings. Don't take him as your paradigm. Don't even receive, or retain, or keep his commandments. For the simple and pure reason that you can, by no means, keep the whole law as he himself did. Forget then definitely the law. Nay, do not even try to do good works. For, at any rate, you do not need them at all for your salvation; rather reject them totally. Thus, believe only in Christ and no matter a saint you are or a sinner and your sins will be washed away by his precious blood; and all things will be right." And so on, and so forth.

Consequently, similar false statements about salvation, emerge leading us to press questioning: aren't these false teachings and

---

[435]-*All the Doctrines of the Bible. Zondervan Books. Grand Rapids, Michigan. Copyright 1964. Page 162.*

fraudulent interpretations of Scriptures that caused America this moral laxity? Isn't this easy and pagan Christianity based upon faith alone in Christ regardless of the reverence and observance of his commandments on Mount Sinai and on Mount of Galilee that weakened the Cristian dogma?

If we can't do good, the whole good; and if we are not able to keep the law, the whole law, because of the weakness and wickedness of our nature per se; and because of the rigorism and rigidness of the static law itself; it does not mean at all that we have to forget, neglect or reject utterly the spiritual law of God embedded in the performance of good works; and do evil instead. And if Paul says, "what I will to do, that I do not practice, but what I hate that I do,"[436] that does not mean either that I have to continue to do the evil I hate, or to cease keeping completely Christ's commandments and "everything will be all right." No, not at all.

Thus salvation is quite and completely contradictory to what heralds haughtily Herbert Lockyer. And using always his own quotations and expressions, I say; "Yes, Salvation is by imitation" indeed, namely:

---

[436]-*(Romans 7:15)*

By "living like Jesus" as Jesus himself did urge us to do, saying, "If anyone desires to come after me, let him deny himself, and take up his cross and follow me."[437] Didn't God himself predestine those who love him, "to be conformed to the image of His Son."[438]

By "imbibing his teachings", yes, as Christ himself exhorted saying, "If you love me keep my commandments.[439]

By "emulating his example"; as Christ himself taught, saying, "For I have given you an example that you should do as I have done to you."[440] As he urged us to be as perfect "as his Father in heaven is perfect."[441] For he and his Father "are one."[442] And as the Apostle Paul in turn wished that the faithful who are Christ's

---

[437]-(Matthew 16:24 and Mark 8:34 and Luke 9:23)

[438]-(Romans 8:29)

[439]-(John 14:15 and 14:21)

[440]-(John 13:15)

[441]-(Matthew 5:48)

[442]-(John 4:15 and Colossians 1:28)

227

Church "should be holy and without blemish,"[443] and that "every man (be) perfect in Christ Jesus."[444]

The Apostle Paul himself invited the Corinthians to imitate him as he also imitated Christ, saying, "Imitate me, just as I also imitate Christ. . . and keep the traditions as I delivered them to you."[445] Isn't that according to such spiritual statements of Christ and Paul that Erasmus wrote his masterpiece, "The Imitation of Christ?" For in such a way only does occur the revival of a very living and lovely Christianity.

Paul also prompted the Philippians to follow his own example too, saying, "Brethren, join in following my example, and note those who so walk, as you have us for a pattern."[446]

He urged Timothy to be, in turn, "an example to the believers in word, in conduct, in

---

[443]-*(Ephesians 5:27)*

[444]-*(Colossians 1:28)*

[445]-*(1 Corinthians 11:1,2)*

[446]-*(Philippians 3:17 and Titus 2:7)*

228

love, in spirit, in faith, in purity."[447] Namely in good works, good deeds, good acts and good conduct.

He also exhorted both Timothy and Sylvanus to become "examples to all in Macedonia and Achaia who believe."[448]

And Peter states, "For to this you were called, because Christ also suffered for us, leaving us an example, that you should follow His steps."[449]

In his Sermon 13, titled, "Christ's People - Imitations of Him" Spurgeon says, "I will endeavor to stir up your minds by way of remembrance, and urge you so to imitate Jesus Christ, our heavenly pattern, that men may perceive that you are disciples of the Holy Son of God". . . and, "A Christian should be a striking likeness of Jesus Christ" and, "We should be pictures of Christ, yea, such striking

---

[447]-(1 Timothy 4:12)

[448]-(Thessalonians 1:7)

[449]-(1 Peter 2:21)

likenesses of him" and, "If you are like Christ, you are of Christ, and shall be with Christ."[450]

As for the other strange statement of Herbert Lockyer, "But Christ after flesh, is not a Savior", I say: "The word, or God, who became flesh"[451] is "the same yesterday, today, and forever"[452] whether before assuming flesh, or after becoming flesh. Namely, Christ is always an eternal Savior.

Salvation has been realized through Christ's very embodiment, teachings, the shedding of his blood, and also "through the life He lived among men." For God, Son of God, and Son of Man, Christ Jesus Himself never ever stopped forgiving sins,[453] and performing miracles, wonders, and signs.

Consequently, Salvation never ever occurred without Christ even in the very past, or "through the life He lived among men" as

---

[450]-*Spurgeon's Sermons. Baker Book House. Volume 1. Pp. 253, 254, 257, 273.*

[451]-*(John 1:14)*

[452]-*(Hebrews 13:8)*

[453]-*(Matthew 9:2 and Mark 2:8 and Luke 5:20 and 7:48 and 23:43 etc.)*

thereafter in all times.

-7-

Yes, it is particularly this very excess of tolerance, indulgence, and leniency on the part of certain religious leaders concerning the observance of the spiritual law of God, that gave free rein even to commit first "small sin", or "good sin" (using Luther's terms); then to commit "big sins"; then to practice immorality and unchastity in consequence.

Isn't it again by this continuous stress and emphasis on the part of some American preachers and teachers of the gospel that "faith alone in Christ" or on "His blood than the Book" as a sole way for salvation, that they are urging and encouraging people to abstain even from doing good works and deeds at all? Aren't they, thereby, pushing them, even to do evil, instead?

Dr. Robert Schuller put it this way: "The strong and not incorrect Protestant emphasis on "salvation by faith, not by works" resulted in hundreds of anti-good-works sermons."[454]

---

[454]-*Self-Esteem: The New Reformation. A Jove Book. Jove Edition. November 1985. Page 162.*

This statement by Schuller reminds me of another one by Billy Graham, although ostensibly not incorrect, but somehow deluding, that says, "A brilliant surgeon to a crusade heard me saying, that if gaining Heaven depended upon good deeds, I wouldn't expect to get there. He had devoted his life to helping humanity, but at that moment he realized his training, his years of hard work, and his love for his profession wouldn't earn him a place with God. This man, who had seen many births himself, knew what it was to be born twice."[455]

Yes indeed gaining heaven or going to heaven, does not depend at all upon good deeds only and solely. And it does not hinge either upon faith alone in Christ regardless of the keeping of his commandments; For Christ himself urged us saying, "If you love me, keep my commandments"[456] and, "If you keep my commandments, you will abide in my love, just as I have kept my Father's commandments and abide in his love."[457]

---

[455]-*How To Be Born Again. By Billy Graham. A Key-Word Book. Word Book Publisher. Waco, Texas. Page 27.*

[456]-*(John 14:15)*

[457]-*(John 15:10)*

232

Nevertheless, a good surgeon, like the good Samaritan, who devotes his life to helping people, loves his profession, trains his years of hard work to do good deeds according to Christ's commandments, is the only righteous Christian who will gain Heaven indeed. "For the just (alone, like this surgeon) shall live by faith."[458] Whereas the "unjust" or the "unrighteous" or the "selfish" surgeon who "devotes his life" to his self-interests and self-esteem only, although a believer in Christ, yet, in consequence, like "demons, who believe and tremble"[459] he will never ever gain Heaven.

For again Justification although granted gratis, is through the very faith of the righteous only in Christ, and not of the unjust or the sinner, unless and until he repents and sins no more.[460]

Even the criminal on the Cross was justified because of his spontaneous sorrow, real repentance, plus a genuine faith in

---

[458]-(Habakkuk 2:4 and Romans 1:17 and Galatians 3:11 and Hebrews 10:38)

[459]-(James 2:9)

[460]-(John 5:14)

Christel.[461] Therefore he was somehow baptized and saved by a single and special function or fiat of Christ's Jesus.[462]

Yet, it seems somehow right to say with Spurgeon, "He that has faith, has renounced his own righteousness.[463] But, on the other hand, he that has no righteousness (or good works) has also renounced totally his faith. For faith and works work in synergism and synchronism so to speak biblically.

Thus, a Christian deprived of righteousness, despoiled of good works, and disposed of good behavior, is a false Christian. And Christianity without the observance of the spiritual law of Christ and the keeping of his commandments, is void, invalid like all other common and countless creeds, cultures and religions. Again Christianity without Christ and the emulation of Christ is a pagan Christianity. "Christianity is a system which helps human beings live the good life; it enables them to engage in right action. Doctrine which has no

---

[461]-(Luke 23:40, 42)

[462]-(Luke 23:43)

[463]-Spurgeon's Sermons. Volume 1. Baker Book House. Grand Rapids, Michigan. Reprinted 1985. Page 381.

moral payoff is useless; piety which fails to express itself in the doing of what is morally right is mere sentimentality or emotionalism."[464]

For again, genuine Christians "are to God the fragrance of Christ among those who are being saved and among those who are perishing,"[465] and not because of the "fragrance" of their <u>invisible and insensible faith,</u> but on the contrary, because of the very scent of their <u>sensible and tangible good works and deeds indeed.</u>

-8-

Some may ascribe excess of immorality in America to the separation of Church and State. For in such a case, they may argue, that the role of Church in caring, cautioning, and controlling, is somehow ineffective or rather obsolete. But on the other hand, didn't Christ himself separate Church and State somehow definitely and beforehand when he pronounced his famous fiat, "Render to Caesar the things

---

[464]-*The Bible in America. Edited by Nathan C. Hatch and Mark A. Noll. Oxford University Press. Copyright 1982. Page 145.*

[465]-*(2 Corinthians 2:15)*

235

that are Caesar's, and to God the things that are God's?"[466]

Anyway, Church and State are well-nigh identical, particularly wherever the overwhelming majority of population is of one belief or religion (As it is the case here in America). Both do not exist by themselves. They are not, thus, two abstract and separate entities, but rather two coexistent popularities in fact and full reality. For the State is the people per se or the very body of citizens. And the Church also is the people per se or the very body of believers. Therefore, despite the principle of religious freedom embodied in the First Amendment of the American Constitution, citizens and believers, as a whole, are somehow the same agglomeration and congregation as well. In fact there is no final and strict separation of Church and State in America. Thus, Church as a private association even though subject somehow to the law of State, is essentially free, and morally obligated to teach righteousness according to Christ's commandments, and to marshal morality into society.

In this regard says W.A. Visser't Hooft, The First General Council of Churches ". . the

---

[466]-*(Matthew 22:21)*

Church is the alter ego of society and society is the alter ego of the Church . . . But the underlying idea is that church and state and society cannot be separated, that they are conterminous and that membership in one of them involves membership in all three."[467]

Therefore, to me, this egregious and strange dissociation on the part of people from Christian ethics, and their penchant for immorality is due, basically, to many factors, and the greatest among them, are the following:

First, the impotence of the High Court of Justice in the implementation of the First Amendment by a fair and correct and courageous interpretation. Namely by a firm Christian interpretation, no more, no less.

Second, the impassivity of the State itself that is Christian, vis-a-vis immorality.

Third, the disinterest of families themselves in rearing and raising their children in the very Christian life and belief.

---

[467]-*God and Man in Contemporary Christian Thoughts. Edited with an Introduction by Charles Malik - American University of Beirut - Centennial Publication 1970 (The Contemporary Church P.1).*

Fourth, the deficiency and lack of Christian education in schools and universities alike while America itself is "under God Christ."

Fifth, the cowardly muteness and carelessness of the clergy itself towards corruption and immorality.

Sixth, the dare deviltry of movies, televisions and videos in the display of:

Horrible and odious retribution almost in all films regardless of God's declaration, "Vengeance is mine, I will repay."[468]

Unlawful and awful sex act.

Extreme violence, savagery and atrocious killing that surpass even ferocious beasts slaughters. In Time Magazine, July 1991, writes Barbara Ehrenreich, "There's something wrong when a $7 movie in the mall can leave you with post-traumatic stress syndrome. In the old days killers merely stalked and slashed and strangled. Today they flay their victims and stash the rotting, skinless corpses. Or they eat them filleted, with a glass of wine, or live and with the skin still on when there's no time to cook.

---

[468]-(Leviticus 19:18 and Deuteronomy 32:35 and Romans 12:19)

It's not even the body count that matters anymore. What counts is the number of ways to trash the body: decapitation, dismemberment, impallings and . . . But. . . The scary thing, the thing that ought to make the heart pound and the skin go cold and tingly, is that somehow we find this fun to watch!"

Yes indeed it is horrifying not to budge, not to blame, not to censure, and not to condemn writers and producers of such filthy films! Even four centuries B.C. murders and crimes, in Greek tragedies, were committed behind closed doors and drawn curtains. That, was done in respect for common sense and not to hurt the human feeling. Thus heathen Greeks were more moral and religious than the so-called faithful of today. And it is because of much gore and slaughter on his stage, the atheist Voltaire called Shakespeare, "the barbarian?"

Now what about our sensational stage, violent movies and permissive televisions?

I leave the response, here too, to the Highest Court of Justice in our Country, to their prudence, jurisprudence and integrity. I leave it to their Christian ethics and education alike.

I also would like to close this chapter by repeating time and again:

That America never stopped or ceased to be a biblical and religious nation, a very "one nation under God." Gary Wills asserts, in an Introduction page 16 to his book entitled "Under God"; and according to reliable references by Gallup and Castelli and other polls and sources that the overwhelming majority of Americans believe in God, Judgement Day and Resurrection; and attend Churches more than sports events.[469]

On one hand, through the dynamic and devout preachers of the gospel, faith is still extant and persistent in America. On the other hand, because of many apostates, corruption is rampant, and faith is waning, and consequently, immorality is flaunting and flourishing day by day. And Scriptures says, "The name of God is blasphemed among the Gentiles because of you."[470]

Briefly speaking, a world without Christ and Christian morality, is a decadent, decaying

---

[469]-*Under God: Religion And American Politics. Simon and Schuster. Copyright 1990. Page 16.*

[470]-*(Romans 2:24 and Isaiah 52:5 and Ezekiel 36:22)*

and dead world indeed, a world reminiscent of the Roman Empire before her fatal fall.

I hope that the peoples of the so-called civilized world, are not heading or rather not hurtling, nowadays, towards that very era of paganism: towards that total licentiousness and decadence.

242

IV
A BLATANT BIG BUSINESS

-1-

Among other dominant factors contributing to the flourishing of various and numerous denominations and congregations in the Protestant Church, (especially nowadays in America) is that the act of preaching and teaching the gospel has also become somehow a conspicuous big business that brings a corresponding big money.

For, to have one's private and profitable business, one must have, of course, his own congregation. And to have his own congregation, one must have also his particular profession and prophecy so to say; and thereby accordingly his private property and prosperity, his very treasury indeed.

Hence also, no preacher, or priest, or evangelist does dare attack or criticize deviations, or deflections, or eccentricities, or in brief, unorthodox teachings of others whosoever and whatsoever. For as the Arabic proverb says, "It's better to cut one's neck than to cut his means of living," i.e., his very business. And as

245

the French adage says, "Everyone for himself, and God for all." Or, in other common and simple terms, "Live, and let others live."

Therefore, no wonder, that the diverse cults and cultures, denominations and congregations in every corner, club, block, lot, center, quarter, mansion and the like are mushrooming; almost always for the sake of the continuous flow and amassing of funds, and of mammon. Priests were wanting at the time of Emperor Charles V, as writes a Spaniard, saying, "I see that we can scarcely get anything from Christ's ministers except for money: at baptism money, at bishoping money, at marriage money, for confession money and, not extreme unction without money! They ring no bells without money, no burial in the church without money; so that it seemeth that Paradise is shut up from them that have no money. The rich are buried in the church, the poor in the church yard. The rich man may marry with his nearest kin, but the poor not so, albeit he be ready to die for love of her. . ."[471] Whereas Paul

---

[471]-*Great Voices of the Reformation. By Harry Emerson Fosdick. A Modern Library Giant. New York. Copyright 1952 by Random House, Inc. The Introduction.*

warned that "bishop" must not be "greedy for money."[472]

Explaining this "universe" of preaching the Gospel in America, the French magazine, Le Figaro, reported Friday 10, 1987, "To better understand this universe, one should go back to the between-two-wars era when curious individuals travelled the Southern States to deliver a revised corrected biblical message. With the start of the TV age, the preachers do not miss the opportunity; first with weekly Sunday programs, then daily, they quickly became overnight superstars with wholesome parts. But to save the world from perils that assail and threaten to sink it, it is necessary of course to send money, more money, to the preacher . . . And dollars to start pouring in, flowing and flooding the Televangelists purses. Thus the institution of considerable empires such a Oral Roberts, empires that stir up vocations that prosper and feed on promising and faltering perspectives.

In the 70's with the speed of Cable TV, tens of millions of homes can be reached at a quicker pace."

---

[472]-(1 Timothy 3:3)

And Le Figaro magazine reported the roughly total sums the following Televangelists earn each year:

Jimmy Swaggart 140 million dollars.
Robert Schuller 70 million dollars.
Pat Robertson 180 million dollars.
Oral Roberts 30 to 40 million dollars.

"Richard Roberts, son of Oral Roberts," Le Figaro says, "inundated the faithful with thousands of letters soliciting donations and ending with this phrase, "Do so, that wouldn't be my dad's last anniversary." It is said that when the sum of 8 million dollars that Oral Roberts claimed was attained, the son, however, didn't stop his postal crusades."

Jimmy and Tammy Bakker 129 million dollars.

Three months before Le Figaro, Time magazine, April 6, 1987 (Section Religion) put it this way, "Counting radio, the gospel broadcasters' total receipts probably approach $2 billion a year. To critics as well as concerned believers, the industry often seems more concerned with bucks than Bibles, and with the personality cults more than the Spirit of Christ. Captivated by the unholy row, newspaper-headline writers christened the improprieties

248

God's cam, God's gate, Heaven's gate, Salvation gate, Pearly gate and Gospel gate."

Both Time magazine issues, February 17, 1986 (under the title "Power, Glory and Politics) and August 3, 1987 (under the title "Enterprising Evangelism") and Le Figaro magazine, Friday, July 10, 1982 (under the title "Ils Ont Casse La Tirelire Du Bon Dieu), mentioned the annual income of some Televangelists, as the following:

Marion Gordon (Pat Robertson) $233 million. And $182 million (for the year ending March 31) or $180 million (according to Le Figaro).

Jimmy Swaggart $140 million or $142 million or $140 million (according to Le Figaro).

Robert Schuller $37 million or $42 million, or $7.6 million per month. And Time magazine August 3, 1987 also declared that "the perpetually upbeat preacher and his staff refused for weeks to cooperate with Time in discovering finances; but last week stated that the ministry had 1986 operating revenues of $35 million and expenses of $31 million." And according to Le Figaro magazine Robert Schuller's annual revenue was $70 million; and it also added, "But nobody knows precisely his income".

Jimmy Bakker $100 million or $5 million per month or $129 million (according to Le Figaro).

Jerry Falwell $100 million or $84 million or $5.6 million per month.

Oral Roberts $120 million or $5.8 million per month.

James Kennedy $20 million.

Billy Graham $66.6 million ("who still gets the highest TV ratings of any preacher for his occasional prime-time crusades").

Herbert W. Armstrong; Chairman of the Worldwide Church of God, "The Armstrong operating fund, is perhaps twice that of the huge Billy Graham Evangelistic Associates, and several times that of the Oral Roberts empire, the only two independent evangelistic organizations of comparable size." And though claiming, "not only refuse to ask for contributions on the air, they also offer their monthly magazine, numerous booklets and Bible correspondence course without charge:

yet, through direct tithes and donations the annual income of this wealthy organization reached $55 million."[473]

-2-

Jesus Christ said, "The laborer is worthy of his wages."[474] Although He himself did not refuse financial help from "Certain women who had been healed of evil spirits and infirmities. . who provided for him from their substance,"[475] however, He never ever appealed for money, or accepted offerings or donations or contributions or the like, in exchange for his teaching or healing. He never ever urged people to finance him by any direct or indirect manners or means or mediums.

Apostle Paul in turn notified saying, "Do you not know that those who minister the holy things eat of the things of the temple, and those who serve at the altar partake of the things of the altar? Even so the Lord has commanded

---

[473]-*The Preachers. By James Morris. St. Martin's Press. New York. Copyright 1973. Pp. 320, 321, 362.*

[474]-*(Luke 10:7)*

[475]-*(Luke 8:23)*

that those who preach the gospel should live from the gospel."[476]

But "to live from the gospel" or "to eat of the things of the temple," is one thing; and to thrive, and treasure, and possess powerhouses and empires, and to turn into a tycoon or magnate or mogul from the gospel is another thing indeed.

Talking about Televangelism, the vocation of preaching the Word of God, and how it became in America a special kind of big business, Time magazine reported August 3, 1987 (under the title "Enterprising Evangelism"), "In less than two decades, the vocation of preaching the Word of God via video has grown from hard scrabble beginnings into far-flung real estate and broadcast empires with assets saying in the hundreds of millions of dollars. In almost every instance, those holdings are dominated by a single dynamic individual who decides how the money will be spent and who strives above all, to keep vital donations flowing from the faithful."

Now the critical and crucial questions here:

---

[476]-(1 Corinthians 9:13,14)

Doesn't the American preacher and teacher of the Gospel (be he a Televangelist, or a simple evangelist or priest on radio, or without television and radio) know this very and simple fact that "it is hard for a rich to enter the kingdom of heaven?"[477]

Doesn't he also remember, rather tremble at, and fear, what the Apostle Paul advocates and states with terrible terms to Timothy, "And having food and clothing, with these we shall be content. But those who desire to be rich fall into temptation and a snare, and into many foolish and harmful lusts which drown men in destruction and perdition. For the love of money is a root of all kinds of evil, for which some have strayed from the faith in their greediness and pierced themselves through with many sorrows."[478]

Isn't he fully aware that to be really and truly Christ's disciple, he has to bear his cross[479] and not his own money box or bank's checks?

---

[477]-(Matthew 19:23 and Mark 10:24 and Luke 18:24)

[478]-(1 Timothy 6:8-10)

[479]-(Luke 13:27)

Didn't Christ himself caution and warn his disciples and apostles in all ages not to "provide neither gold, nor silver, nor copper in (their) belts, but rather to deliver freely the message they got freely?[480] Meaning, purely and simply, to deliver it gratis, without charge, and free of cost. Otherwise, any Christian message delivered in exchange for money, or any kind of donation, or contribution, or offering is ipso facto called simony[481] that is "applied to all traffic in spiritual offices."

Didn't Isaiah herald, inviting people to abundant life, "Ho! Everyone who thirsts, come to the waters; and you who have no money, come, buy and eat. Yes, come, buy wine and milk without money and without price?"[482]

Oh! How admirable would have been the mission of these preachers and teachers of the Gospel, if their money belts, boxes, and banks were somehow empty of gold, silver, copper, and dollars as that of their Lord Jesus Christ! For, even to pay the simple temple tax, Christ himself should seek a piece of money in

---

[480]-*(Matthew 10:8,9)*

[481]-*(Acts 8:20)*

[482]-*(Isaiah 55:1)*

the mouth of a fish.[483] And that because he used to distribute the contents of his box to the destitute and the needy; or to buy with, things his disciples needed;[484] another good reason, perhaps, that egged on Judas Iscariot to betray him for thirty pieces of silver.[485]

How wonderful would have been, if they themselves, once receiving generous donations and offerings with one hand, were in turn, giving them with the other hand to the poor and to social and cultural benefits! As some of them are doing so silently, sincerely, and very gladly "for God loves cheerful givers."[486] Although rich, maybe richer than Abraham and Job, some of these pious and generous American preachers, are not less at all than Abraham and Job, in their faith and righteousness. Because, "with man it is somehow impossible that a rich man to be saved, but with God all things are possible."[487]

---

[483]-(Matthew 17:24-27)

[484]-(John 13:29)

[485]-(Matthew 6:14)

[486]-(2 Corinthians 9:7)

[487]-(Matthew 19:26)

Besides, although these preachers and teachers of the Gospel lack the power of their Lord and God Jesus Christ, in providing money "from the mouth of a fish," as he himself did, yet, as highly educated, they can easily manage and live even without any sort of salaries or stipends or wages, or the like from the faithful. They can for instance preach in churches, and teach in universities, and do many other respectable and profitable businesses for some specific salaries. Their primary paradigm should be Christ himself, who used to practice carpentry. Their other paragon, Paul, was a tent maker[488] and he, himself, testifies saying, "I have coveted no one's silver, or gold, or apparel. Yes, you yourselves know that these hands have provided for my necessities, and for those who were with me. I have shown you in every way, by laboring like this, that you must support the weak. And remember the words of the Lord Jesus who said, 'It is more blessed to give than to receive.'"[489]

-3-

To someone who said to Jesus, "Teacher, tell my brother to divide the inheritance with

---

[488]-(Acts 20:33)

[489]-(Acts 20:33-35)

me", Jesus answered him saying, "Man, who made me a judge or an arbitrator over you?"[490] And that because Jesus Christ mission was spiritual from beginning to end.

For the sake of great wealth, most of the American preachers and teachers of the gospel, are interfering deliberately, almost in every spiritual and material matter as well: In the social and in the individual; in the public and in the private; in the sacred and in the secular; in the familiar and in the formal, and so on, and so forth.

Consequently, they are judges, arbitrators, physicians, psychiatrists, counselors, consultants, businessmen, clergymen, sociologists, pharmacologists; theologians and commentators on the Scriptures, pretending that they know all their secrets and mysteries.

They also own stores and storages, houses and warehouses, shops and workshops, clinics and offices that are fully equipped with all sorts of treatments, medicaments, drugs and diverse devices; and, with special miraculous verses "clichés" from both the Old and the New Testaments.

---

[490]-*(Luke 12:13,14)*

Therefore, here too, they are constantly available, most often from behind their microphones or telephone number, or through their diverse and numerous publications, to deal with every case, heal every disease, resolve every dilemma and every enigma. And they are available every time of course, in exchange for whatever sum of money, or contribution, or donation, or tithe, or the like.

But the most funny thing is that, they are taping most of their commentaries, sermons, and precepts and prescriptions, plus their secular and pragmatical sciences, in series of cassettes and tapes. Moreover, they are dripping them so to say in small doses, very small doses: As in piles, or pills, or drops. They are also storing them in turn, in countless cassettes, tapes and records. Most often, for example, a short and clear biblical verse, lengthily explained, is extended and sometimes wrongly interpreted, is put into one single cassette. At some other times, a sole and simple terminology (like "truth," or "faith," or "sin" or "grace" for instance) thoroughly and exhaustively explained and interpreted, is inserted in series of cassettes!

Thus, infinite cassettes are dedicated for infinite verses, terms, terminologies, topics and types of problems from both the Old and the

New Testaments. Each cassette, for example, is sold for five dollars or more. Infinite publications, rife and replete with similar topics and secular subjects alike, are sold every day in exchange for millions and millions of dollars.

And now, imagine the infinite divine mine of gold, silver, copper, and dollars in which, these modern preachers and teachers of the Gospel are digging and drawing from! And imagine now, how many different and costly cassettes, books and booklets should the faithful buy to satiate their hunger, and quench their thirst for the Word of God and salvation!

To put some of their good teachings and correct commentaries in cassettes, tapes, records, books, booklets and pamphlets is not bad at all. Rather it is, sometimes very important and profitable if distributed gratis. But to sever, for example, and set apart, a biblical terminology or verse which is very comprehensive impressive and meaningful once in their won context and proper place; and then explain them very exhaustively and thoroughly; and insert them in series of cassettes or tapes or books and booklets is somehow a malign marketing. (Whereas, some of the best recorded sermons, in certain churches, are delivered to the faithful free of cost or sold three dollars per cassette, i.e., less maybe than their very costs price indeed).

Moreover, aren't their own teachings, precepts, prescriptions, advices, commentaries, etc. etc. surpassing thus, in number and oppressiveness, even the 613 commands and commandments of the Mosaic law itself?

Now again, pause and ponder the poor folk of Christ, how, where, and when (In the present life or in next) can they digest all this severe nourishment for salvation?

Aren't they, thereby, loading the faithful with burdens very hard to bear as Scripture states, "Woe to you also, you lawyers! For you load men with burdens hard to bear, and you yourselves do not touch the burdens with one of your fingers."[491]

All this reminds me of a certain Roman Emperor who killed his guests very much like in a Hitchcock movie (in manner and style). The funny anecdotes reports that this maniac-Emperor, invited his guests to a lavish banquet set inside a luxurious rotunda. Then after he gave orders to lock hermetically all its doors, entries and accesses; piles of aromatic petals

---

[491]-*(Luke 11:46)*

were poured over the cheerful guests from the dome's openings as an apparent gallant gesture and generous hospitality of their Emperor; until all his guests were exultantly suffocated.

-4-

When Jesus said to the multitudes and to his disciples, "Whatever they (the scribes and the Pharisees) tell you to observe, that observe and do,"[492] he certainly didn't mean to observe their own false and deceitful teachings that he himself so impugned and castigated.[493]

However, nowadays, while the Holy Bible is available to everyone, and most of the people are literate, why, then, are these modern preachers and teachers of the Gospel, depriving the faithful from its fullness and abundance? Why aren't they instigating them to read and reread it constantly? And why are they feeding them their own fantastic teachings and the crumbs of their complicated commentaries instead? Why is, then, Christ so capsulated in

---

[492]-*(Matthew 23:3)*

[493]-*(Matthew 16:3-20 and 23:16-33 and Mark 7:6-23)*

261

cassettes? And why costly cassettes instead of Christ who died gratis even "for the ungodly?"[494]

Besides, by constant computerized letters and pitiful petitions, modern and very rich preachers and teachers of the Gospel themselves, be they telecasters or broadcasters, are begging money, always more money for the supposed supporting of their missions, missionaries and so-called crusades. As, of course, for the sustenance of their crews, cronies, and courtiers as well. In this regard, says Time Magazine, February 17, 1986, "Preachers who purchase air time frequently offer books, calendars, lapel pins and whatnot to those who phone or write in. Viewers requesting "premiums" often send checks, but the preachers' real goal is to build a computerized name list for future direct mail solicitation."

And mostly, these preachers are soliciting money plus prayer, especially from the poor. Because purely and simply the poor are pure in heart, (not to say silly and gullible) and good believes, and consequently good donors indeed.

---

[494]-(Romans 5:7)

To your dismay, you may marvel here and say, "Wow! O irony of ironies! Have you ever heard millionaires and multimillionaires praying poor's indulgences and prayers together?"

But consider, once again, the vast numbers of the poor wherever they are, and the considerable amounts of money collected from their regular tithes, donations and contributions, and you will certainly discover, to your amazement and anger now, how clever, cunning, and clairvoyant also are these "ravenous wolves"[495] wherever they are!

Time Magazine, August 3, 1987, under the title "Enterprising Evangelism" (Section Religion) put it this way, "The ratings changes are highly significant in the Televangelism industry, because viewers form what ministries term their "donor base." The faithful TV audience is a mainstay of ministry income providing a steady flow of gifts, commonly $10 or $20 a contributor. The name and addresses of donors are carefully preserved in computer banks and used in direct mail donation pitches, another major source of ministry income. At the Jimmy Swaggart Ministries headquarters, for example, workers used to extract some $2.5

---

[495]-*(Matthew 7:15)*

million in monthly donations from occasional donors."

In old times, tithes were brought usually into the common store house or treasury of the Lord,[496] or to the Temple in Jerusalem.[497] And from there, Tithes were distributed to the Lord's ministers and servants.[498] But nowadays, money is brought to every preacher's bank and treasury.

-5-

No, I am not at all against a wealthy Church, or a rich Congregation, or an affluent and opulent Mission. For to supply support for the needy, send missionaries elsewhere, build churches, found schools, universities, and seminaries, and the like, Churches and Congregations and Missions, should be richly rewarding and not only to survive but to satisfy, succeed and excel indeed. Neither am I a poverty preacher nor praiser. For poverty per se is neither a virtue nor a vice once coercive, compulsive, and forcible. "Give me neither poverty nor riches" says Proverb 30:8. To saint

---

[496]-*(Joshua 6:19 and Malachi 3:10)*

[497]-*(Matthew 12:41 and Luke 81:1)*

[498]-*(1 Corinthians 9:13,14)*

John Chrysostom, "Poverty is not a virtue per se, but rather necessity, exigency, pain and agony."[499]

But I am against the extravagant wealth of clerics, individuals and families, who somehow suppress and withhold the Word of God. Yes I am against this pseudo-evangelist, the very mogul who monopolizes by himself so to speak the apostleship juggernaut in the name of Christ.

For, no, not a single person among Christ's disciples or apostles in all times reached the opulence and extravagance of some of these modern American Evangelists and preachers of the Gospel. Are we then "in the last days and perilous times" in which "men (no matter clergymen they are or laymen) will be lovers of themselves, (the cult of self-esteem) lovers of money, boasters, proud, blasphemers, disobedient to parents, thankless, unholy, unloving, unforgiving, slanderers, without self-control, brutal, despisers of good, traitors, headstrong, haughty, lovers of pleasure rather

---

[499]-George Florofsky, "John Chrysostom, prophet of love," from aspects of Church history. Arabic translation by Fr. Michel Najim, Al-Nour, 1980, page 136.

than lovers of God, having form of godliness but denying its power?"[500]

-6-

The Apostle James says, "If a brother or a sister is naked and destitute of daily food, and one of you says to them, "Depart in peace, be warmed and filled," but you do not give them the things which are needed for the body, what does it profit?"[501]

And to my very disappointment, this was exactly the response of a well noted pastor and preacher on radio, to a certain similar destitute of James. By sobs, supplications, and humiliation, the poor "brother" (in Christ) was exposing and expressing his touchy case as a jobless, hopeless, and very needy. And the very noted preacher and teacher of the Gospel on radio, only by sweet words did he sermonize and satiate him, just before jumping and leaping to another sweet call of a certain lady on the air. For, besides occasional faithful, almost all his devout listeners and followers are females who do solicit him to resolve always, from behind the microphone, their diverse

_____

[500]-*(2 Timothy 3:1-5)*

[501]-*(James 2:15,16)*

266

psychological and neurotic problems and puzzles, in exchange for their steady contributions and generous donations of course, and the purchasing of his publications and numerous and various cassettes that deal with all their problems and heal all their sicknesses.

Aren't these acts, manners, and means of preaching and teaching the Gospel nowadays in America, somehow a terrific traffic in spiritual offices, rather as I said before, a stupendous simony?

How, then would Luther himself, the father of Protestantism, have reacted towards such a tremendous religious traffic? Wouldn't he have labelled such a flagrant selling (tax deductible, of millions and millions of publications, cassettes, books, booklets, brochures, pamphlets, posters, and many other diverse and devilish devices, and so-called religious trinkets and trifles, yes, for many and many millions of dollars) even worse than the historic Bulls and Indulgences of his time?

268

V

A PSEUDO-REALM FOR PSYCHIATRY AND PRAGMATISM

"Christ came to bring everyone the joyous, exuberant, pulsating life that makes Him so winsome."

"I am not getting any younger. You conduct a personal problem clinic to study people and you have had some experience, and I am putting my problem right up to you. Tell me, why can't I get married?'

Norman Vincent Peale
(The Power of Positive Thinking)

-1-

To procure people health and wealth, happiness and success, self-esteem and salvation as well, most of the American preachers and teachers of the Gospel, not only do consecrate their mission, consume their thinking, but blend boldly religion and science, Christology and psychology, eschatology and psychiatry as never ever done before with the whole history of Christendom.

Dr. Norman Vincent Peale says, "...it is my conviction that the principles of Christianity scientifically utilized (meaning that in the entire Christian era they were either non-utilized scientifically or badly or wrongly utilized) can develop an interrupted and continuous flow of energy into the human mind and body."[502]

And to "corroborate these findings" by Mrs. Edison's answer to his request that "His (Thomas Edison) relationship with the universe

---

[502]-*The Power of Positive Thinking. Prentice-Hall Press. New York. Copyright 1987. Pp. 30, 31.*

caused nature to reveal to him its inscrutable secrets," Dr. Peale concludes triumphantly as by Archimedes' Ureka, "Every great personality I have ever known, and I have known many, who has demonstrated the capacity for prodigious work, has been a person in tune with the infinite. Every such person seems in harmony with nature and in contact with the Divine Energy. They have not necessarily been pious people, but invariably they have been extraordinarily well organized from an emotional and psychological point of view."[503]

Now, in these two above mentioned statements of Peale, we notice four non-biblical and non-scientific ideas as well:

First, his conviction "that the principles of Christianity can be utilized scientifically" is a false conviction, because Christianity does not deal directly and solely with man's worldly problems like health, wealth, success, happiness and the like, but rather, and specifically, with salvation of his soul and his redemption from sin. In other words, "principles of Christianity" do deal directly and drastically with human final fate, future, and fortune after death according to his faith, and good or bad works and deeds. Even though with scientific reasoning we can,

---

[503]-Ibid. Page 32

sometimes, discover, some biblical truth even objectively, yet, science and religion inherently, are by no means, in harmony: "The Bible is always fresh and thoroughly "up to date." Indeed it is far, far ahead of human science. Progress cannot overtake it or go beyond it. Generation succeeds generation, but each finds their Bible waiting for it with its ever fresh and never failing stores of information touching matters of the highest concern, touching everything that effects the welfare of human beings".[504]

Second, this "tuning with the infinite" is not Christian at all, but rather a Buddhist pantheism that teaches that God and the whole world are one and the same thing. In other words, according to Buddhist Pantheism God does not exist as a self existent, or a separate Spirit. Whereas the Gospel declares clearly, "God is Spirit."[505]

Third, "Harmony with nature," like "tuning with the infinite," like "contact with the Divine Energy" or God, all this is a mere and

---

[504]-*The Bible in American. Edited by Nathan O. Hatch and Mark A. Noll. New York. Oxford University Press. Copyright 1982. Page 144.*

[505]-*(John 4:24)*

275

sheer rhetoric and literature and not theology. Besides, all this is totally opposite to what the Scriptures teach. For no one can "contact" God, or "tune" with God, or comprehend God by any sort of Zen, or meditation, or contemplation, or the like. It is by Christ Jesus alone that we can contact, and comprehend God: "I am the way, the Truth, and the life. No one comes to the Father except through me."[506]

Fourth, it is naive and non-scientific to say that "His (Thomas Edison) harmonious relationship with the universe caused nature to reveal to him its inscrutable secrets."
Francis Bacon says, "The subdue nature, we must obey it." Meaning, to allow nature reveal to us its "inscrutable secrets," rather its "physical and natural laws," we have to accept, before all else, its very facts and phenomena, observe them carefully (and not romantically), and yield to the understanding of their causes and effects. And thereby only, we can deduce the very scientific laws of nature, as did Edison, Newton and long before them the Greek mathematician and inventor Archimedes (13th Century B.C.) and others. Here too, Pasteur says (19th Century), "Hazard does not favor but prepared minds." Meaning that the "inscrutable secrets of nature" are revealed only to scientific men and

---

[506]-(John 14:6)

women who constantly muse and meditate, probe and ponder them. Consequently, sometimes, all of a sudden, those "inscrutable secrets" are disclosed to them. But, never, ever, by the simple act of "tuning" or "coping," can a barber, for example, discover a scientific law, or a scientist "run a beauty parlor," if you please.

Yes, indeed, Christ is Christ of Scripture and Science simultaneously, of heaven and earth alike. But, it is not necessary at all that perspicuity and lucidity of nature, should absolutely confirm and contend the lucidity and perspicuity of Scripture; and vice versa.

Also proclaims Peale, "In our brains we have about two billion little storage batteries. The human brain can send off power by thoughts and prayers. The human body's magnetic power has actually been tested. We have thousands of little sending stations, and when these are tuned up by prayer it is possible for a tremendous power to flow through a person and to pass between human beings. We can send off power by prayer which acts as both a sending and receiving station."[507]

This extravagant and bizarre statement of Dr. Peale is also a simple and servile

---

[507]-*The Power of Positive Thinking. Page 53*

reverberation of what Frank Laubach did advocate in his book, (Prayer, The Mightiest Power In The World), "I regard this (book), says Peale, as one of the most practical books on prayer, for it outlines fresh prayer techniques that work. Dr. Laubach believes that actual power is generated by prayer. One of his methods is to walk down the street and "shoot" prayers at people. He calls this type of praying, "flesh prayers." He <u>bombards</u> passers-by with prayers, <u>sending out</u> thoughts of good will and love. He says that people passing him on the street as he "shoots" prayers at them <u>often</u> turn around and look at <u>him</u> and smile. <u>They feel the emanation of a power like electrical energy</u>. In a bus he "shoots" prayers at his fellow passengers. . . Dr. Laubach believes that he had often changed the entire atmosphere of a car or bus full of people by the process of "swishing" love and prayers all around the place."[508]

Applying Dr. Laubach's "prayer techniques", and "shooting prayers," and "bombarding" of passenger and passersby "with prayers;" and his "process" of "swishing" love and prayers, etc. etc, Dr. Norman Vincent Peale, in turn emulated Dr. Laubach and contends and confirms that he himself practiced them very successfully. He cured, for instance,

---

[508]-*Ibid. Page 52.*

as he pretends, an alcoholic. "One Tuesday, he recounts, about four o'clock, he "started praying for him". . . He prayed "about a half hour." And to make a long story short, exactly at that very moment, i.e., on Tuesday, at four o'clock, the alcoholic was healed. How? He "went to a drugstore, bought a box of candy, and ate all of it without stopping. That pulled him through, he declared- "prayer and candy."[509]

Now, all these so-called "emanation of prayer power," "flashing," and "swishing prayers," and "shooting," and "bombarding" prayers like "electrical energy," are neither biblical nor scientific, but rather, sad to say, satanic and mere and sheer pretensions and deceptions. For both Laubach and Peale here, are suggesting the simple and the gullible, that they are performing miracles and wonders as Jesus himself did, and somehow in the same way. Didn't, for instance, a power get out from Jesus, and healed "a woman, having a flow of blood" at the very moment she "came from behind and touched the border of his garment?"[510] And the nobleman who "implored Jesus" to heal his son who was "at the point of death," didn't the fever leave him "at the

---

[509]-Ibid. Pp. 53, 54.

[510]-(Luke 8:43-46)

seventh hour?" i.e., exactly "at the same hour in which Jesus said to him, "Your son lives!?"[511]

But Christ Jesus, is the omnipotent, and the omniscient, and the omnipresent God Himself. Whereas Peale and Laubach are common men, endowed with "special" gifts, and "magnetic power" as they pretend. Scripture says, "pray for one another, that you may be healed. The effective, fervent prayer of a righteous man avails much."[512] However, effectiveness, and ardency, and power of prayer are not due to the "human brain" per se that "can send off power by "thoughts and prayers" as Peale and Laubach allege. But rather, prayer request is made or addressed to God only; and God alone, who accepts prayers, can perform accordingly miracles of healing and curing as well as other wonders and signs.

Peale also says, "I again understood why Jesus Christ retains his remarkable hold on men. It is because He has the answer to such problems as these (namely as tension or stress, or being "a bundle of excitable and explosive nerves", or the like), and I proved that fact. . . I began to recite certain Bible texts such as,

---

[511]-(John 4:46-53)

[512]-(James 5:16)

"come to me all ye that labor and are heavy laden, and I will give you rest,"[513] and, "Peace I leave with you, my peace I give to you; not as the world gives, do I give to you. Let not your heart be troubled, neither let it be afraid."[514]

Then Dr. Peale claims that, by reciting "these words slowly, deliberately, reflectively" he noticed his (patient) or "visitor" who was "too tense, too high-strung, that (he) fumed and fretted too much," then "stopped being agitated. Quietness came over him." And Dr. Peale infers here, "No, not the <u>words</u> <u>alone</u>...though <u>they</u> <u>do</u> <u>have</u> <u>a</u> <u>remarkable</u> <u>affect</u> <u>upon</u> <u>the</u> <u>mind</u>, but something deeper happened just then. He touched you a minute ago, the Physician (Christ) with the healing touch. He was present in the room."[515]

Up to now, especially in this final conclusion, Dr. Peale seems to be truly a genuine and fantastic Christian, and somehow a very pious man. For Christ the omnipresent is always present, especially "where two or three

[513]-*(Matthew 11:28)*

[514]-*(John 14:27)*

[515]-*Ibid. Pp. 79, 80.*

are gathered together in His name". He is, yes, "in the midst of them."[516]

But what is deceiving on the other hand, in Peale's statements and arguments, is his first saying, ". . . I again understand why Jesus Christ retains his remarkable hold of men. It is because He has the answer to such problems." And the answer of Christ to such problems according to Peale also, was Christ's sayings, "Come to me, all ye that labor etc." and "Peace I leave with you." etc. As if Christ's Power of healing was not in his proper person per se as an omnipotent God, but rather in his specific "answers" (or "words") themselves to "such problems," in such touchy situations. As if any other human being, like Peale and others, can use such clichés fiats or formulas, and heal thereby people. And as if Jesus himself, like Peale, was also a "founder of religio-psychiatric clinic institutes for Religion and Health, and Guide posts magazine" (See the back flap of his book "The Power of Positive Thinking) and, for "spiritual rules for developing and retaining confidence, techniques for achieving material and emotional success. . . methods to sustain a maximum in energy level. . . program for eliminating worry" (also on the back flap).

---

[516]-*(Matthew 18:20)*

Yes, it is quite right and very biblical also when Peale attests, "No, not the words (of Christ) alone" cured the "prominent citizen of New York" whose "power resources (were) played out,"[517] but "the Physician (Christ) with the healing touch: He was present in this room" (i.e. in Peale's clinic). But it is deceiving to the people and distorting to the Scriptures themselves, when Peale suggests that if Christ's "statements" or "ideas" or "dictums" or "words" were "used scientifically" as "spiritual rules, or techniques, or methods" etc. by themselves alone (i.e. without Christ's direct presence or interference, or the belief in him as the very God and sole Savior) that may heal people or "have a remarkable effect upon the mind."

Thus, to Peale, "Faith per se, i.e., belief, positive thinking, rather than faith in God (namely here, traditional God) and faith in other people, faith in yourself, faith in life, is what makes miracles.

Thus, again, "This is the essence of the technique that teaches." "If thou canst believe", it says, "all things are possible to him that believeth."[518] "If ye have faith. . . nothing shall

---

[517]-*Ibid. Page 79.*

[518]-*(Mark 9:23)*

be impossible unto you."[519] Believe - believe - so it drives home the truth that faith moves mountains."[520]

And "faith" here, to Peale, is of course, and as usual, "faith in other people" or "faith in yourself" or "faith in life" and the like. This is indeed a perversion of the faith. He forgets here and there, and always intentionally, the core and kernel of Christ's teaching and clear statement: "for without me you can do nothing"[521] and the Apostle Paul's, "I can do all things through Christ who strengthens me."[522]

Peale also says, "Students of modern dynamic thought are realizing more and more the practical value of the ideas and teachings of Jesus, especially such truths as the dictum "according to your faith, be it unto you."[523] Dr. Peale goes on to say by adding, to our dismay and amazement, his own and proper dictums, "According to your faith in yourself, according

---

[519]-(Matthew 9:29)

[520]-Ibid. Pp. 87, 88.

[521]-(John 15:5)

[522]-(Philippians 4:13)

[523]-(Matthew 9:29)

to your faith in your job, according to your faith in God, (always his traditional God. But in Matthew 9:29, it was according to the faith of the "two blind men" in Jesus himself who said to them, "Do you believe that I am able to do this?" that "their eyes were opened" and not in their "own faith" or faith in the abstract and traditional God of Peale and others) this far will you get and no further. If you believe in your job and in yourself and in the opportunities of your country...you can swing up to any high place to which you want to take your life and your service and your achievement."[524]

And the responses to these extravagant, confusing, biblical and secular statements of Peale is:

First, Christ's sayings, "Come to me, all you that labor and are heavy laden, and I will give you rest" and "Peace I leave with you, my peace I give to you, not as the world gives, do I give to you," are in direct contradiction of Peale's false interpretations of Scriptures. For Christ's sayings do not attempt to solve only and solely momentary and worldly problems such as tension, stress, nervousness and the like, as Peale suggests.

---

[524]-Ibid. Page 92.

Secondly, Christ's other saying, "According to your faith, be it unto you," is not at all a "dictum" i.e. a simple principle, or proposition, or opinion. It is rather the "very faith" in Christ himself as the sole God who alone can perform the miracle of healing the blind[525] and all other sicknesses and weaknesses, and even the raising of the dead. These false, fake, and fraudulent faith "in yourself," or in "your job," or "in the opportunities," or "in your country," as preaches and teaches Dr. Norman Vincent Peale, (These latter "faiths") are rather simple and common "confidences" imparted to all human beings, each one according to his courage or cowardliness, no more no less.

Third, this particular faith in Christ is the sole mean for salvation of the soul and not a pragmatical "instrument" or "technic" or "rule" or "method" through which "you can swing up to any high place to which you want to take your life and your service and your achievement" as Dr. Peale states and suggests.

Fourth, it is again by faith in Christ alone "who strengthens me (that) I can do all things,"[526] and not by faith in myself, or in any

---

[525]-(Matthew 9:29)

[526]-(Philippians 4:13)

286

other forces or persons in the world. For it is Christ Jesus himself who said, "Truly, truly I say to you, he who believes in me, the works that I do, he will do also; and greater works than these he will do."[527] However, he asserted also saying, "For without me you can do nothing."[528] This means that our own confidence per se is fruitless; and our own faith in our selves or in other powers of the world is futile and vain indeed (i.e., in the realm of the real miraculous, the supernatural and the pure divine). For faith, real faith, true faith as defined by Paul "is the substance of things <u>hoped for</u>, the evidence of things <u>not seen</u>." It is this same faith that he confirms in Hebrews Chapter 11:1-40; Paul concentrates on Christ Jesus alone, "the author and finisher of our faith."[529]

Peale also says "to a young woman who couldn't get married, ". . . nowadays we have to cover the whole field in a human problem." Then, it is only by his advice, and in his own "office," that she "put into practice the principles (he) suggested (and) applied the spiritual technics" or "formula;" and accordingly,

---

[527]-*(John 14:12)*

[528]-*(John 15:5)*

[529]-*(Hebrews 12:2)*

she got married thereafter. And Peale added, recounting this funny episode, "she had evidently visited God's beauty parlor" (a new "technic" or "formula" of his "old professor at Ohio Wesleyan University, "Rolly" Walker who said, "God runs a beauty parlor.") "He (his professor) explained that some girls when they came to college were very pretty, but when they came back to visit the campus thirty years later their beauty had faded. The moonlight - and - roses loveliness of their youth did not last. On the other hand, other girls came to college who were very plain, but when they returned thirty years later, they were beautiful women. "What made the difference?" he asked, "The latter had the <u>beauty</u> of <u>inner</u> <u>spiritual</u> <u>life</u> written on their faces". . . "God runs a beauty parlor."[530]

Without denying the beauty and serenity "of inner spiritual life" written (sometimes) on (some) faces of saints and genuine Christians, we have to admit, that "inner spiritual life" can be also written <u>on</u> <u>emaciated</u> <u>and</u> <u>lean</u> <u>faces</u> of another category of saints and righteous men and women, such as John the Baptist who used to live in the wilderness feeding on "locusts and wild honey;"[531] and the Apostle Paul, the globe-

---

[530]-*Ibid. Pp. 91, 92 .*

[531]-*(Matthew 3:4 and Mark 1:6)*

trotter who disciplined and subjected his body,[532] and Mary Theresa who has been sacrificing her entire life for serving the sick, and the destitute; and many, many others.

Thus, real righteousness and sanctity are not necessarily reflected always on sturdy faces and surfaces alone. They are rather embedded in good behavior, godly life, decent character, and good deeds. But, alas, "the moonlight - and -roses loveliness" of youth and beautiful faces, sooner or later will fade and vanish as the prophet says, "All flesh is grass, and all its loveliness is like the flower of the field. Surely the people are grass, the grass withers, the flower fades, but the word of God stands for ever."[533]

Departing from the saying of Christ, "If you have faith as a grain of mustard seed...nothing will be impossible for you,"[534] Dr. Norman Vincent Peale deceptively deduces saying, "Faith even as a grain of mustard seed will solve your problems, any of your problems, all your problems, if you believe it and practice

---

[532]-*(1 Corinthians 3:27)*

[533]-*(Isaiah 40:5-8)*

[534]-*(Matthew 17:20)*

it. <u>Little</u> <u>faith</u> (even less than a grain of mustard seed?) gives you little results, (like what?) <u>medium</u> <u>faith</u> gives you medium results. (!!!) <u>Great</u> <u>faith</u> (bigger than a grain of mustard seed?) gives you great results (like what here too?).

Digressing and deluding, as if to correct himself, Peale mixes as usual religion with secular pragmatism, by adding, "But in the generosity of Almighty God, if you have <u>only</u> the faith symbolized by a grain of mustard seed, it will do amazing things in solving your problems."[535]

And the question here is: why all this "much ado about nothing," if the sole goal and purpose is to, transmit, and substitute "faith in Christ" for "little," "medium" and "great" faiths in the abstract and traditional "Almighty God," then, for faith "in yourself," or "in your job" or "in the opportunities" or "in your country;" then, for his "pseudo-technics, and formulas of well-being"? As if faith in Christ is a common confidence like all other self - and - pseudo-confidences of men?

Now again, to refute Dr. Peale's pseudo-preaching and philosophical teaching of

_____

[535]-*Ibid. Page 133.*

"success" based (as he pretends) on Paul's statement, "I can do all things through Christ who strengthens me"[536] I say, in a terse tale: "Yes, Christ does strengthen all those who, like Paul, do love Christ, keep his commandments, bear his cross, and emulate his life style and deeds. Therefore, my question, here, to Dr. Peale is:

"Can he sincerely proclaim like Paul, "Imitate me, just as I imitate Christ. . . and keep the traditions as I delivered them to you?"[537] Or prompt us as Paul prompted the Philippians themselves to follow his example, saying, "Brethren, join in following my example, and note those who so walk, as you have us for a pattern. For many walk, of whom I have told you often, and now tell you even weeping, that they are the enemies of the cross of Christ: whose end is destruction, whose good is their belly, and whose glory is in their shame-who set their mind on earthly things?"[538]

And if so, yes, he (Dr. Peale) can "do all things."

---

[536]-(Philippians 4:13)

[537]-(1 Corinthians 11:1,2)

[538]-(Philippians 3:17-19)

But again, can he really? I strongly doubt it.

-2-

Like his very paradigm Norman Vincent Peale, Dr. Robert H. Schuller declares in the first page of his Introduction (to his book "Self-Esteem: The New Reformation") his secular view and vision that contradict squarely the Scriptures, saying, "Perhaps, we are at an era where psychiatric and religious thinking can be synergistic." Meaning that Religion, and here Christianity, is somewhat incapable by itself to achieve its role (of course, for salvation) unless and until it is supported by psychiatry; and vice versa.

And the direct response to such a claim is: No. Never ever. For, semantically, religion differs totally from psychiatry. By definition, Religion is "the service and worship of God or the Supernatural" (First definition in Webster's New College Dictionary). And Christianity is "the Christian religion, founded on the teachings of Jesus" (The American Heritage Dictionary). Whereas psychiatry is "the medical study, diagnosis, treatment, and prevention of mental illness" (The American Heritage Dictionary) or "A branch of medicine that deals with mental, emotional, or behavioral disorders" (according to Webster's New Collegiate Dictionary).

Therefore, Christianity deals with ethical values, i.e., with human virtues and vices, righteousness and wickedness which engender either eternal life in heaven (If man is a believer in Christ and keeper of his commandments) or eternal damnation in hell (If man, on the contrary, is a continuous sinner and non-believer in Christ).

Consequently, psychiatric and religious thinking, can by no means or meanings be synergistic or synergic. They are rather mutually antagonistic from beginning to end: "Most Christians have failed to recognize the fact that Christianity and psychotherapy are actually two rival and irreconcilable religious systems. Their union as "Christian psychology" creates an unequal yoke that brings into the Church the seductive influence of secular psychology."[539]

Time Magazine, March 18, 1985 also reports, "Like his early model positive thinker Norman Vincent Peale, Schuller combines an affirmative outlook withhold fashioned piety to

---

[539]-*The Seduction of Christianity. By Dave Hunt and T.A. McMahon. Harvest House Publications. Eugene, Oregon. Copyright 1985. Page 30.*

assure his audiences that self-esteem and success are desirable and achievable. During an hour that sometimes resembles a celebrity talk show, Schuller speaks earnestly of the alluding desire of self-worth of "every person's deepest, one's spiritual hunger for glory."[540]

And the most stunning and deceiving thing, is to see Dr. Schuller distorting even the very meanings of Scriptures themselves for the sake of success and self-esteem of individuals. He says for instance, "God's plan and purpose calls for us to succeed and not to fail. "I am the vine, you are the branches. He who abides in me. . . bears much fruit." Here then is our definition of success. To succeed is to "bear fruit" i.e., to be productive. . . We must, therefore, never stop believing in success. For when we succeed, all of society will benefit (just the contrary is right). There will be no success without a cross. As a result, the self-esteem generates enthusiasm" (en theos, "in God", i.e., a branch that is abiding in the vine!). And Robert Schuller concludes, "May God hear and answer our prayers and protect us from the temptation to seek success without the cross."

No, "to bear fruit" and "to abide in Christ", is not at all, "to succeed and be

---

[540]-*Self-Esteem: The New Reformation. P. 120, 121.*

294

productive" in Schuller's secular sense and false interpretation of Christ's statement. But rather to have more morality in the practicing of righteousness through Christ himself and by his guidance and help. For "without Christ we can do nothing."[541] Matthew Henry commenting on this verse, put it in a very correct way, "we must be fruitful. From a vine we look for grapes, and from a Christian we look for Christianity; this is the fruit, a Christian temper and disposition, a Christian life and conversation. We must honor God, and do good, and this is bearing fruit. The disciples here must be fruitful, as Christians, in all the fruits of righteousness, and as apostles, in diffusing the savior of the knowledge of Christ."[542]

Therefore, "bearing fruits" is not "to be productive" in the sense of being materially rich and cultivating one's cult of success, self-esteem, or by "running public beauty parlors."

Christianity, if properly appropriated and fairly managed and manipulated, is not against science, success, health and wealth. For Christ himself also said, ". . . seek first the Kingdom of

---

[541]-*(John 15:15)*

[542]-*Commentary on the Whole Bible. Zondervan Publishing House. Grand Rapids, Michigan. Copyright, 1961.*

God and his righteousness, and all these things shall be added to you,"[543] and, "Truly, truly I say to you, there is no one who has left house or parents, or brothers, or wife, or children, for the sake of the Kingdom of God, who shall not receive many times more in the present time, and in the age to come everlasting life."[544] And Matthew Henry comments on this statement of Christ, saying, "No man has left the comfort of his estate or relations for the Kingdom of God's sake, who shall not receive manifold more in this present time, in the pleasures of communion with God and of a good conscience advantages which will abundantly countervail all their losses."

-3-

In the "manners", "methods", and "technics" of Dr. Vincent Peale and Dr. Robert Schuller, many other American preachers and teachers of the gospel are pragmatic and consciously materialistic. They endeavor earnestly and before all else, to solve urgent and earthly problems of their followers; their mental, physical and social problems. Furthermore, they strive to ease their strains

---

[543]-*(Matthew 6:32)*

[544]-*(Luke 18:29,30)*

296

and stresses, and assuage their tensions and alleviate their emotional problems. In brief, they attempt to make them more confident in their lives, more successful in their jobs, and happier. As if success and happiness in this world only, are all they need. As if by bread alone man lives in America. But concerning the world to come; and life after death and its final destiny, they most often refrain from talking about, lest they impede or imperil their followers' feelings and temporary success; lest they harm and hamper their happiness on earth, nowadays. As if nowadays is the only lifetime on earth as well as in heaven.

"Success is the name of the game today, not only out there in the world, but inside the Church as well. Success and self-esteem have become so important in the Church that they seem to overshadow everything else."[545]

But is it not too long before Peale and Schuller (precisely in the year 1955) that "Oral Roberts or Brother Roberts who published one of his most successful books, "God's Formula for Success and Prosperity" was reissued in

---

[545]-*Ibid. Pp. 14,15.*

1966"[546] paving thereby the way widely for them by focusing on preaching success, health, happiness, and wealth on earth, instead of laying up "treasures in heaven"[547] as Christ taught?

Thus, instead of insisting on:

Putting the stress and emphasis on:

Meditation day and night in the spiritual law of God[548] and the observance of his commandments on Mount Sinai[549] and on Mount of Galilee.[550]

Reciting without ceasing the Lord's prayer,[551] and praying constantly[552] so that God forgives our sins and trespasses and deliver us

---

[546]-*The Preachers. By James Morris. St. Martin's Press. New York. Copyright 1973. Page 109.*

[547]-*(Matthew 6:19,20)*

[548]-*(Psalm 1:2)*

[549]-*(Exodus 34:28 and Deuteronomy 4:13 and 10:4)*

[550]-*(Matthew 5:1-27)*

[551]-*(Matthew 6:9-13)*

[552]-*(Luke 21:36 and 1 Thessalonians 5:17)*

from the evil, troubles and tribulations of the world.

Reading periodically and permanently the Holy Bible (and particularly the New Testament). For, "How many mysteries are solved in it, how many revealed!"[553]

Studying diligently the Scriptures in the light of genuine commentaries of the first Father of the Church; and reading the authentic and authoritative translations of the Bible, and neglecting, rather rejecting translations and interpretations and comments and commentaries pertaining to the radical theologians who in the name of freedom and individuals' views and insights, mutilated the truth and distorted the Scriptures themselves.

Attacking zealously, constantly, and severely false doctrines that mushroom almost every day in many denominations (As the Apostle Paul did diligently).

---

[553]-*The Brothers Karamazov. Fyodor Dostoevsky. Translated by Andrew H. MacAndrew. Bantan Books. Copyright 1981. (Book VI: A Russian Monk - page 351)*

Fasting,[554] and Fleeing "youthful lusts and pursuing righteousness, faith, love, peace with those who call on the Lord out of a pure heart"[555] and fleeing "sexual immorality."[556]

Repenting, confessing, and performing repeatedly good acts, deeds and works according to Christ's commandments.[557]

And Urging people to attend regularly the Church, and partake of communion as it was the continuous habit of the first and foremost faithful[558] and as it is up to date the habit of the overwhelming majority of Christians in the world.

Yes, instead of preaching that, preachers and teachers of the Gospel of the New Age are rather:

---

[554]-(Matthew 17:21 and Mark 9:29 and Luke 2:37 and Acts 10:30 and 14:23 and 1 Corinthians 7:5 and 2 Corinthians 6:5 and 11:27)

[555]-(2 Timothy 2:22)

[556]-(1 Corinthians 6:18)

[557]-(John 14:15 and 14:21 Matthew 5:19 and 7:24)

[558]-(Matthew 26:26-28 and Mark 14:22-24 and Luke 22:7-20)

Inciting their congregants to buy and read and concentrate on their own publications, most often, a farrago of biblical, psychological, psychiatrical, philosophical, pragmatical advices, precepts and prescriptions.

Soliciting money, lots of it, from their pulpits and platforms.

Suggesting to the faithful, that their own teachings, advices, attractive announcements and fantastic remedies are:

Fabulous formulas for the acquisitions of prosperity and power.

Keys and insights for success, successful, joyful and bountiful living on earth and in heaven.

Indispensable remedies for the controlling and curing of surfeit, sorrow, anguish, ennui and anxiety.

Easy, safe, and wonderful ways for celebrity, security, and self-esteem.

Sure and suitable solutions for the removal of remorse and inferiority-complex.

Effective efforts for calming and silencing the sense of sin and guilt (especially for redivorced and remarried men and women).

Secure and serviceable systems for satisfaction of self-desire, pride, and hunger for health, wealth and happiness.

Practical rules and pragmatical regulations for the ultimate success in business, and the developing of confidence in all aspects of life.
Brand new Methods and Mores for the improvement in interpersonal relations, and achievements of high and desirable goals in life.

Efficient and sufficient means for positively thinking, sensing, acting and behaving.

Particular and practical means to overcome obstacles, conquer fear, dispel despair and renew hope of happiness and full confidence in life.

Inspirational influx of self-confidence, vitality, and prodigious power not only to survive but to succeed and excel. And so on, and so forth.

As all these pragmatical precepts and worldly wisdoms are of course supported and sustained by particular prayers, beneficial blessings and fervent requests from pastors, preachers and teachers of the gospel.

Yes, all that again:
As if man is born to live in the world only.

As if the present world is man's final abode; forgetting that Christ himself warned us saying, "Do not labor for the food which perishes, but for the food which endures to everlasting life, which the Son of Man will give you, because God the Father has set His seal on Him."[559]

As if self-esteem, self-pride and self-success are the ultimate and sole goal of man on earth; and consequently, "Let us eat and drink, for tomorrow we die."[560]

-4-

Yes, it is good and profitable to acquire in this world methods, rules and technics for the achievement of material success; and the surmounting of momentaneous stress; as well as for the eliminating of sorrow, sadness, worry,

---

[559]-*(John 6:27)*

[560]- *(Isaiah 22:13 and 1 Corinthians 15:32)*

fear and the like. But to fasten all our hope upon these only, isn't like focussing upon worldly cares and concerns alone? Isn't it contradicting also, the task of every preacher of the gospel who put the emphasis, only on psychiatry and psychology, and not on salvation of the soul after death. "For what is a man profited if he gains the whole world, and loses his own soul? Or what will a man give in exchange for his soul?"[561]

Napoleon Bonopart has this motto to brandish and brag, "My head is like a closet with many drawers. Every time I go to bed to sleep quietly, I put every problem that bothers me in its drawer, and sleep like a plank."

Quoting this motto of Napoleon, I said once in one of my short stories entitled, "Priority's right," "could the boastful Emperor put Waterloo in its drawer, at least the first night he slept in Saint Helena Island?" For as says Goeth, the German author, "The human nature has its limits; once these limits are over-flowed, man succumbs."

Therefore, no "positive thinking," or adamant will, or the so-called "energy in human brain," can by themselves overcome the

---

[561]-*(Matthew 16:26)*

unsurmountable, or sweeten the unbearable. Nor can they divert or discard or escape juggernauts that are beyond man's capacity.

And among all calamities and misfortunes, death is the most puzzling, frightening and frustrating. All other human problems, compared to it, are futile, trivial and insignifcant indeed. Although everyone wants to eke out every fraction of his life, death does put an end to all our aspirations, endeavors and hopes.

Influenced most probably by the parable of the "Rich man and Lazarus" in Luke 16:26, Shakespeare says (In Hamlet Prince of Denmark, Act III Scene I):

> "But that dread of something after death,
> The undiscovered country, from whose bourn
> No traveller returns - puzzles the will,
> and makes us rather bear those ills we have."

But it is Christ alone, the omnipotent God, who hopefully "returned" and made others return from that "undiscovered country".

Says the Apostle Paul, "And if Christ is not risen, then our preaching is vain and your faith is also vain. . . If in this life only we have hope in Christ, we are of all men the most pitiable. . . But now Christ is risen from the dead and has become the first fruits of those who have fallen asleep."[562]

Christ alone said emphatically, "I am the resurrection and the life. He who believes in Me, though he may die, he shall live. And whoever lives and believes in Me shall never die."[563] For Christ, at his second and final coming to earth, will put definitely an end even to death itself as says Paul also, "The last enemy, that will be destroyed is death."[564]

Furthermore, it is Christ himself who gives us a warning that there is something much more dreadful even after death, that sinners will be punished and perish in hell: "And do not fear those who kill the body but cannot kill the soul. But rather fear Him who is able to destroy both soul and body in hell."[565]

---

[562]-(1 Corinthians 15:12, 19, 20)

[563]- (John 11:25, 26)

[564]-(1 Corinthians 15:26)

[565]-(Matthew 10:28)

Do preachers and teachers of Positive Thinking, think about this very fact, i.e. "Life after death" as all Scriptures do teach and exhort them to do so?

Yes indeed, all our spiritual, mental and serious physical problems are due, mostly to our pleasure, unfaithfulness, greediness and hatred; namely to our sins. Says James, "Where do wars and fights come from among you? Do they not come from your desires for pleasure that war in your members? You lust and do not have. You murder and covet and cannot obtain. You fight and war. Yet you do not have because you do not ask. You ask and do not receive, because you ask amiss, that you may spend it only on pleasures."[566]

Therefore, it is not through any philosopher or psychiatrist or positive thinker that we have to look for the healing of our spiritual and mental sicknesses. Nor should we seek for the security of our minds, and the serenity of our souls, through the teachings and technics of such preachers-psychiatrists. No, not at all. It is rather, through Christ alone we are soundly secure, and saved. It is by continuous reading and meditating in his gospel, and the keeping of his commandments, that all our

---

[566]-(James 4:1-3).

problems are solved: "Come to me, Jesus said, all you who labor and are heavy laden, and I will give you rest."[567]

Under the big title "Pope urges convert Drive, even where Moslems ban it," the New York Times International, Wednesday, January 23, 1991, reports the following, "John Paul also had harsh words for the modern world and it "soulless economic and technical development," a world of "marvelous achievements that nevertheless seems to have lost his sense of existence itself. "The temptation today is to reduce Christianity to merely human wisdom, a pseudo-science of well-being" he said.

-5-

After I quit school for the long haul, and precisely, for a period that spanned twelve years, I got married. And having five children, I pursued anew my studies first at home in order to complete the second part of the baccalaureate (philosophy branch); then at a local university for the Master of Arts (in philosophy also). Our professor (General Philosophy and Psychology) was an unmarried priest in his forties: paunchy, with a strong face and trimmed black beard. His malicious eyes

---

[567]-(Matthew 11:28)

308

and smile reminded me always of Leonardo Da Vinci's Backus; and his protruding pot belly, of the sybarite Sant Beuve's statement, "Rejoice my belly, for everything I earn is for your sake." The first day he entered our class I whispered to a close and brilliant friend sitting next to me, "Can philosophy engender such a belly as his?" And my intuition wasn't wrong. For, besides his bookish imagination and shallow knowledge of both philosophy and psychology, he was a real frank liberal and daredevil. To illicit laughter from few coeds in our class, sitting in front of his pulpit, he used to crack the most indecent jokes that I personally cannot even repeat to others.

Aware of my observance of and allegiance to Christian morality (By way of his cousin, a classmate, and through a special speech he asked me once to deliver in class, in which I quoted twice the Apostle Paul) he asked me ironically at the end of the graduation's year, and before all my colleagues, "Thomas, now that you are somehow well informed about Evolution and Existentialism, psychology and psychiatry; and have somewhat good understanding of the trio; Freud, Adler and Young; are you still sticking to your classical theology?"

My friends burst into laughter. And I said, first, to myself, "Oh the presumptuous priest and empty clergyman!"; then openly, ironically, and minutely, "Most reverend pastor, and respectable Professor, all that you have taught us, as you know, are mere theories that contradict, each other, abolish, in a way each other, and in consequence, are obsolete."

My friends burst again, but with boisterous and even longer laughter. "Therefore, I continued very calmly, I can claim afresh with more emphasis that I am now, much more on safer ground, attached much more to Christian morality, and have much stronger inclination to my classical theology, if you please."

VI

A DEMONSTRABLE DISPLAY FOR
PERFORMANCE AND HILARIOUSNESS

"Truly, truly I say to you, they have
their reward."
(Matthew 6:2, 5, 16)

-1-

To please people, most of the American preachers and teachers of the gospel, are competing in the displaying of their abilities of oration and rendition, stylization and sophistry so to speak. Thus, instead of delivering Christ directly, and in the very simplicity and sincerity of Scriptures, they are rather hiding him behind the exhibition of their own performance and grandiloquence, psychiatry and rhetoric, and the like.

Do you really want to present Christ to the world? Then do not intercept him by the opacity of your pompous personality and bombastic style and wittiness. Disappear, eclipse, so that Christ alone shines forth. Do as John the Baptist did when he presented him for the first time to the multitudes saying, "I am not Christ. . . I am the voice (a mere voice only) of one crying in the wilderness, "Make straight the way of the Lord. Whose sandal strap I am not worthy to lose. . . He must increase and I must decrease. . . He who comes

315

from above is above all."[568] Yes, preach Christ in the very simple, sincere, and straight forwardness of his first and foremost dsciples and apostles; and for instance of Saint John Chrysostom in the 4th century; and in the 20th century in the very simplicity and sincerity and efficiency of E. Stanley Jones who preached the Gospel in India for a long time, and Billy Graham after him, as like him, in America amd worldwide for more than fifty years up to date.

Dr. James Stalker put it this way: "The preacher who is afraid of his audience, and respects the persons of the learned and the great, is thinking of himself and of what will be said of his performance. But he who feels himself driven by a divine mission forgets himself. All audiences are alike to him, be they gentle or simple; he is thinking only of the message he has to deliver."[569]

Paul says to the Galatians, "For do I persuade men of God? Or do I seek to please men? For if I still pleased men, I would not be

---

[568]-(John 2:30-36)

[569]-Jernican Press 2048N. Druid Hills Rd.N.E. Atlanta Georgia, 30329. Copyright 1981. F.L. Jernigan. Page 73.

a servant of Christ."[570] And addressing the Corinthians, he writes, "And I, brethren, when I came to you, did not come with excellence of speech or of wisdom declaring to you the testimony of God."[571] And, "We knew that we all have knowledge. Knowledge puffs up, but love edifies."[572] And, "For our boasting is this: The testimony of our conscience that we conducted ourselves in the world in simplicity and godly sincerity, not with fleshly wisdom but by the grace of God and more abundantly toward you."[573]

Although sitting in Moses' seat, the scribes and the Pharisees were also teaching, besides God's law and commandments, their own false and deceitful doctrines (or "leaven") as Jesus labelled their teaching; warning moreover his disciples to take heed of it.[574]

But the most saddening, is to see, even nowadays, many of the so-called apostles of

---

[570]-(Galatians 1:10)

[571]-(1 Corinthians 2:1)

[572]-(1 Corinthians 8:1)

[573]-(2 Corinthians 1:12)

[574]-(Matthew 16:6)

317

Christ, behaving like the scribes and Pharisees of old. For they are boastfully blending God's word with their worldly wisdom, exploiting thereby the Scriptures themselves for their self glorification and prosperity, nay, to be called Professors, Doctors, Psychiatrists, Psychologists, Philosophers and the like; exactly like the Scribes and the Pharisees who were craving "to be called by men" Rabbi, Rabbi."[575] James Morris reports it in this ironic way, "Critics who brought up the Old Southern saying, "Most fundamentalist preachers never find peace of mind until they can call themselves "Doctor" or start their own Bible school."[576] As some of these Televangelists do not refrain even from the fixing of their flagrant and flaming title "Dr. X, Ph.D." on the front of their pulpit (at their churches themselves) to be seen even on the TV screen.

-2-

And to amuse and relax their audiences, nearly all the American preachers and teachers of the Gospel, are mustering up all their skills of cracking jokes, lots of jokes; and exhibiting

_____

[575]-*(Matthew 23:7)*

[576]-*The Preachers. St. Martin's Press. New York. Copyright 1973. Page 110.*

their talents by telling anecdotes, many funny anecdotes.

No, I don't say that the using of jokes and pleasant anecdotes while sermonizing or preaching the Gospel or writing religious books, is unfair or indecent. No, not at all. I am rather in favor of pleasant parables and didactic anecdotes that are sometimes very desirable and profitable as well.

For even Jesus talked and taught in such potent parables. Concerning John the Baptist, he once used this enjoyable and cordial comparison: He likened the generation of his time to "children resting in the market places and calling to their companions, and saying, "We played the flute and you did not dance; we mourned to you, and you did not lament." For John came neither eating nor drinking, and they say, "He has a demon." The Son of Man came eating and drinking, and they say, "Look, a gluttonous man and a wine bibber, a friend of tax collectors and sinners." And here, I deem, some in the multitudes who heard him, smiled, and others, maybe, roared with laughter. But when Jesus, continuing, added, "But wisdom is justified by her children,"[577] many also, I

---

[577]-(*Matthew 11:16-19 and Luke 7:31-35*)

presume, though scowled and scared, were awe-stricken.

The Apostle Paul, in turn, did not refrain, sometimes, from using seriocomic jokes and even caustic comments in his letters, as elsewhere. For instance, he said to Ananias, the high priest who "commanded those who stood by him to strike him (i. e., Paul) on the mouth," "God will strike you, you white washed wall" (How the English translation here, with the succeeding and sonorous "Ws" is impressive, suggestive, and figurative as well!). And here also, I think, some of the audience smiled or laughed secretly at Paul's response. But when Paul added, "For you sit to judge according to the law, and do you command me to be struck contrary to the law?"[578] even Ananias and those standing by him, felt ashamed and maybe shivered from fear, for they judged him unjustly.

As among Paul's most sardonic and sarcastic statements is his saying to the Galatians quarreling with one another, "But if you bite and devour one another, beware lest you be consumed by one another."[579]

---

[578]-(Acts 23:2,3)

[579]-(Galatians 5:15)

320

Thus, using humor, and integrating decent jokes and didactic anecdotes while sermonizing or preaching and teaching the gospel, might turn momentary amusement and laughter into contemplation, contrition, and sincere sorrow. Otherwise, as says Solomon, "It is better to go to the house of mourning than to go to the house of feasting. . . Sorrow is better than laughter, for by a sad countenance the heart is made better. The heart of the wise is in the house of mourning, but the heart of the fools is in the house of mirth."[580]

But the excess of cracking jokes and telling funny anecdotes and amusing insights in the churches, in purpose to please people and make them laugh boisterously and hilariously, and even say hysterically, is not only regrettable but abominable. It is rather exactly like the setting "in the seat of the scoffers" as says David in the first verse of his first Psalm.

For frequently, such strange loud bursts of laughter in God's houses make most of worshipers forget the bottom line of the preacher's sermon, and recall particularly his magniloquence, amusing jokes, theatrical performance, refined style and sophistry. Indeed, you most often hear, once outside the

---

[580]-(Ecclesiastes 7:3,4)

church after such tremendous and joyful audiences, the similar following dialogue between buoyant groups:

Q: How was the sermon today?

R: Truly, I don't know. . . I mean I don't remember exactly its details. But by the way, wasn't the preacher, as usual, fantastic? Magnificent?

Q: He was really tremendous! Terrific! Wasn't he?

Then both begin, each in turn, to relate and reiterate the funny anecdotes and jokes of their prodigious preacher; and to comment on his wittiness and cleverness of speech, and to burst laughing again and again. Yes indeed, it is those jokes and joyous talks themselves (of the preacher) that ruled out somehow the spirituality of his sermon. No, no doubt about that. The prodigious preacher did succeed indeed by making his audience happy, very happy for another day of a lovely life on earth. In any case, wasn't that all he wanted to do? Wasn't his conspicuous concern to amuse them, and gain their consent, and thereby the continuous flow of money whose love "is a root of all kinds of evil,"[581] and of scandals alike as reports Time Magazine, February 17, 1986, "The preachers' fund raising, the stuff of jokes and sometimes of scandal is prodigious?"

And to comfort and satisfy people, nearly most of these preachers of the New Age, avoid very strictly and skillfully even the naming of "God" by "Christ," or of "Christ" by "God." They rather preach the abstract and traditional God, instead, in their sermons and publications. And that of course, in the sole purpose to please nominal Christians and Non-Christians as well. But Christ's tremendous warning, "For whoever is ashamed of me and my words in this adulterous generation, of him the Son of Man also will be ashamed"[582] will thunder for ever in their consciousness and subconsciousness.

As they eschew intentionally the mentioning of terrific terms and statements in Scriptures that depict everlasting torments of sinners in hell. Then they most often refrain from relating, particularly the frightening passages in St. Paul's epistles that state categorically, "Do you not know that unrighteous will not inherit the Kingdom of

---

[581]-(1 Timothy 6:10)

[582]-(Matthew 8:38)

323

God? Do not be deceived. Neither fornicators, nor idolaters, nor covetous, nor drunkards, nor revilers, nor extortioners will inherit the Kingdom of God,"[583] and the like. Yes, they abstain from mentioning these statements of Paul lest they hurt their followers' feelings; lest they damage them emotionally, psychologically, and physically. Sadly enough they exactly do what is diametrically opposed to Scriptures: They do preach them salvation gratis through Christ's compassion and love, regardless of any definite and decisive repentance on their part, or any good works or good behavior or good conduct. As if sin per se, is something very normal and natural; and salvation, in consequence, is inevitable and always bestowed without any charge. And if so, then again, "let us eat and drink, for tomorrow we die."[584]

Thus, to assuage the very sense and sting of sin and remorse, these pseudo-preachers and teachers of the gospel, always promise salvation gratis through sweet Jesus' blood, grace, forgiveness, clemency and limitless mercy; regardless of keeping constantly Christ's commandments; and regardless of repentance as Jesus himself exhorted sinners saying, "Sin no

---

[583]-(1 Corinthians 6:9,10)

[584]-(1 Corinthians 15:32)

more, lest a worse thing come upon you,"[585] and "Neither do I condemn you; go and sin no more."[586]

Aren't these preachers, by the way, the very lecturer of oratory and magniloquence, of merriment and entertainment alone?

At any rate, they are neither willing to evangelize nor to proselytize, but rather to please and placate people of all races, religions and ranks. Consequently, "they have their reward."

---

[585]-*(John 5:14)*

[586]-*(John 8:11)*

EPILOGUE
THE SAINTED SYNTHESIS

I do admit, that I personally have no right to judge; for the Lord says, "Judge not, that you be judged;"[587] And as Paul states, "Who are you to judge another's servant?"[588] And, "Therefore let us not judge one another anymore, but rather resolve this, not to put a stumbling block or a cause to fall in our brother's way."[589]

Nor have I the creative and daring imagination of the Italian poet, Dante Alghiery (14th century) to classify, here and there, heretics and schismatics, seculars and pagans, liberals and libertines, syberites and hedonists and sinners of all sorts; and to categorize them, each, in a specific circle in hell.

---

[587]-(Matthew 7:1)

[588]-(Romans 14:4)

[589]-(Romans 14:13)

But rather, regarding preachers of the gospel, I enjoy reiterating with the Apostle Paul, the very architect of Christendom,

"Some indeed preach Christ even from envy and strife, and some also from good will: The former preach Christ even from selfish ambition, not sincerely, supposing to add affliction to my chains; but the latter out of love, knowing that I am appointed for the defense of the gospel! "What then? Only that in every way, whether in pretense or in truth, Christ is preached; and in this I rejoice, yes, and will rejoice."[590]

For, finally, and in any case, the work of all, and particularly of these preachers and teachers of the gospel, these so-called "Televangelists, the stars of the electronic church, the pastors of "Pray TV,"[591] and others be they telecasters, or broadcasters, or simple pastors in their own churches, or offices, or clinics behind their microphones; yes, indeed, their very work will be evaluated, "Each one's work, as says Paul here too, will become manifest; for the Day will declare it, because it

---

[590]-(Philippians 1:15-18)

[591]-Time Magazine, February 17, 1986. (Section Religion)

will be revealed by fire; and the fire will test each one's work, of what sort it is. If anyone's work which he has built on it endures, he will receive a reward. If anyone's is burned, he will suffer loss; but he himself will be saved, yes as through fire."[592] Meaning that God, on judgement day, will reward or punish each preacher of the gospel according to his good or pernicious preaching, his faithfulness or his faithlessness and fraudulence.

However, all pseudo-preachers, who are distorting the Scriptures, and deceiving people by their false teachings and bad behavior, will never be saved if they don't repent, renounce their heterodoxy, and refrain from their apostasy.

-2-

Now, as in the Council of Chalcedon (451), after long, harsh, and bitter contentions, controversies, and haggling over the one or the two natures of Christ, the antagonists said almost the same thing, although in different ways, terms and expressions; likewise also, nearly most of the American preachers, pastors and ministers in the numerous and various denominations and congregations, seem to say,

---

[592]-(1 Corinthians 3:13-15)

somewhat the same fundamental things about the crucial creeds and critical matters of the Bible. For to most of them, if not to all.

Christ Jesus is God and Son of God and the sole Savior of mankind.

God the Father, and God the Son, and God the Holy Spirit are one Godhead or the Holy Trinity.

The Law of God "is holy, and the Commandments holy and just and good."[593]

The unrighteous and all those who do not respect, revere, and keep God's commandments on Mount Sinai and on Mount of Galilee, can by no means inherit the Kingdom of heaven.

To most of them, if not to all, if salvation was possible by the practicing of good works alone, or the observance of the law only, the coming of Christ to the world would not be necessary.

And to most of them, although by Christ alone we are saved, good works should be the only fruits of every Christian. For if Christ, on

---

[593]-*(Romans 7:12)*

his part, did sacrifice himself for our sake; we in turn, should be as saintly and as holy as he is, and that through our faith and good works accordingly.

Therefore, to me, some of confessional differences (around the theoretical so to speak) that split the Churches in the past, did not and could not, however, separate between true Christians themselves, or diminish their faithfulness and devoutness to Christ, no matter what denomination, or congregation or community they belonged to.

Yes indeed, Churches did split in the past ensuing quarrels, controversies and misunderstandings among church hierarchs. Whereas, no one and nothing could wrest, or wrench, or rob the faithful, whoever, from Christ.

Furthermore, to me, those scholastic debates and theoretical disputes and discussions and with their decisions, resolutions and outcomes in the past, were somewhat forgotten thereafter and buried in consequence, inside the neglected publications and the obliviousness of documents (on shelves) in which they were registered.

Therefore, we expect, approve, and applaud enthusiastically every council and councils of churches, that reconvene, and resurrect antique quarrels and controversies (with all their theoretical and nonbiblical conclusions,) but in the sole purpose to rebury them in solemn and final funeral processions.

Before being a compilation of regulations and rigid rituals and rites; and before being a static religion, Christianity is embodied in Christ himself and his dynamic, living, and lovely teachings and commandments. Christianity is embedded in soul and spirit alike, in good conduct, good behavior, and good works altogether.

Hence, all objectives and motives of all ecumenical councils and conventions in the future must be centered around the main Christian faith. It should focus primarily and primordially, on what is unifying churches and not on what split and separated them in the past.

And what unifies churches, is the ruling out categorically, and systematically, all "demoniac denominations" of all sorts whatsoever. Paul says vigorously and rigorously to the Corinthians, "Now I say this, that each of you says, "I am of Paul", or "I am of Apollos", or "I am of Cephas" or "I am of Christ", Is Christ divided? Was Paul crucified for you? Or were you baptized in the name of Paul?"[594]

For Christ Jesus did not send to the world prelates or potentates or Doctors or Psychiatrists or Seers of sees" and "seats," for the purpose of erecting diverse and divisive earthly kingdoms, or Dominions, or Denominations; but rather he delegated simple men, meek men, and humble men to preach his gospel, and settle down his own kingdom in hearts.[595]

So no wonder, if up to date, no one in the long series of all Patriarchs of Antioch reached or rose to the level of St. Ephrem (4th Century) who was a simple deacon; who refrained, and rather refused to be ordained even as a monk. And thus, he deserved the utmost titles and ranks; he was called, "The harp of the Holy Spirit." The Apostle Peter was a fisherman. Paul was a tent maker eating bread "by the sweat of (his) face"[596] and not by faces of other people to the end of his life.

---

[594]-(1 Corinthians 1:12,13)

[595]-(Luke 17:21)

[596]-(Genesis 3:19)

Even Christ himself, was a common carpenter. For "God has chosen the foolish things of the world to put to shame the things which are mighty."[597]

Thus, true believers and genuine Christians in all times, and in all denominations and congregations, are, and have been always "the poor in spirit," and "the pure in heart,"[598] and consequently, the very "members" of the "body of Christ, of his flesh and of his bones."[599]

Therefore, even when Dostoyevski, in his "Diary of A Writer" portrays his own people, the Russian people, he is in a sense portraying also all other common Christians of the world. Says Dostoyevski in this respect, ". . . even though our people do not know prayers, nevertheless the essence of Christianity, its spirit and truth, are conserved and fortified in them. . . despite their vices, as strongly as, perhaps, in no other people in the world. This "deprived" and ignorant people of ours loves the humble man and God's holy fool; in all their traditions and legends the people have

---

[597]-(1 Corinthians 1:23)

[598]-(Matthew 5:3,8)

[599]-(Ephesians 5:30)

preserved the belief that the weak and the humbled, unjustly suffering for Christ, will be raised above the eminent and the strong when God's judgement and ordainment are pronounced. Our people revere the memory of their great and humble hermits and saints; they are fond of reciting to their children the stories about the great Christian martyrs. They have learned and know these stories, and it was from them that I first heard them; they were told with deep understanding and reverence, and they became engraved in my heart."[600]

Billy Graham in turn, believes in the genuine faith of such simple Christian people. Reports Time Magazine, November 14, 1988, "When the post-glasnost Graham preached last June at Orthodox and Baptist churches in Kiev, the authorities allowed outdoor loudspeakers for the overflow crowds, numbering in the thousands. During the Soviet adventures, he added admiration for the Eastern Orthodox to his longtime friendship toward Roman Catholics. "I find the Lord's people among all these groups" remarks Graham, whose toleration infuriates Fundamentalists."

---

[600]-Translated and annotated by Boris Brasol. New York, George Braziller 1954. Copyright 1949 by Charles Scribner's Sons. Page 631.

Now, is it sufficient to say, "to (keep) the faith"[601] in all its fullness, forcefulness, and faithfulness to Christ Jesus, and to keep his commandments, that all other so-called conflicts, contentions, divergences, and diverse doctrines inside the Protestant Church of America, as well as in all other churches of the World, (be they Catholics and Orthodox) be considered, somehow irrelevant? Or rather be accepted as natural signs and symptoms of their spiritual dynamism, health, and improvement? As it is the case of every living and lively church indeed. For only static churches, and stationary religions, and rigid laws, and rigorous rituals, are undeniably dead churches, dead religions, dead laws, and dead rituals; and that because they are based on "the oldness of the letter,"[602] "for the letter kills, but the Spirit gives life."[603]

Luther P. Gerlach and Virginia H. Hine, as reports George Marsden in his book, Evangelism And Modern America, put it this

---

[601]-(2 Timothy 4:7)

[602]-(Romans 7:6)

[603]-(2 Corinthians 3:6)

way, ". . . success of religious movement can actually spring from organizational fission and lack of cohesion. They argue for the inherent dynamism of certain reticulate religious movements - those that are web like, with parts tied together not through a central point but through intersecting sets of personal relations and intergroup linkages. Splitting, combining and proliferating can be seen as clear signs of health. Such movements are superb at recruiting new members and offering the individual a keen sense of personal access to knowledge, truth, and power."[604]

If so to some extent, I do sincerely hope that these seeming negative aspects of preaching and teaching the gospel in America, and particularly this ostensible materialistic marketing of the Word of God that prevail nowadays in its Churches, are accidental, fleeting and thereby, hopefully ephemeral.

For even though each congregation or denomination or Church in Protestantism in America comprehends and interprets some of the crucial matters and mysteries of the Bible, somehow differently, and sometimes even contradictory, one thing is sure and certain, as I

---

[604]-*William B. Eerdman's Publishing Company. Grand Rapids, Michigan. Copyright 1984. Page 77.*

said before, and like to reiterate and assert here: Their Christ is still the same one omnipotent, omnipresent, and omniscient God of the Bible, and the sole Savior of mankind."

Now, the moot question here is: if through computerized and electronical brains, we could separate and select, collect and compile all accurate sermons, genuine publications, authentic and accredited Christian creeds, and true theological treaties, and reliable commentaries on the bible and the like that the Protestant preachers of the gospel are credited for launching throughout their long history up-to-date, wouldn't Protestantism be, verily and truly, if not exactly, the very Catholic and Orthodox churches combined? Or at least, their very equal sister in Christ indeed?

For, it suffices, on the other hand, to count the decent, prominent, and brilliant figures of Protestantism, in the past, as well as recently, who preached Christ Jesus "from good will", (using here Paul's term and testimony) that their reward be great in heaven[605] and that, despite some of their somehow knowingly or unknowingly, grave or great false teachings.

---

[605]-(Matthew 5:12)

Therefore, we can repeat and reiterate with Paul, "what then? Only that in every way, whether in pretense or in truth, Christ is preached; and in this I rejoice, yes, and will rejoice."[606]

For great Figures and Voices of Protestantism, undeniably accomplished grandiose endeavors and good works in the field of Christ Jesus, following are few examples:

They delivered as I related before many accurate sermons, authentic publications, genuine commentaries on the Bible, excellent and stupendous testimonies according to the very core and kernel of Christ's teachings.

They converted innumerable people to Christianity in the five continents.

They certainly participated in the shaping and bettering of our present civilization.

Their life style and good behavior, became, irrefutably, a paramount pattern for millions and millions of people in the world.

---

[606]-*(Philippians 1:18)*

They left their own Christian stamp and seal on many countries where pure Protestantism has been preached.

As it is, undoubtedly, due to their teaching and preaching of the gospel, America, particularly, became the greatest Christian bastion, the wealthiest Nation, and the mightiest power in the world. George M. Marsden says, "America, Protestants held, was founded on the Bible, on Scriptura sola. Without respect for the Bible at the highest level, intellectually and socially, the health and destiny of the nation would be hopelessly damaged. The heart alone, in this nation born of the Enlightenment, was not a sufficient on firm enough ground for intellectual certainty. Science, too, had to be revered. The God of science was after all the God of Scripture. . ."[607]

-4-

Therefore, I presume this Great Nation, America, that two centuries ago, (July 4, 1776 the anniversary of the adoption of the Declaration of Independence by the

---

[607]-*The Bible In America. Edited by Nathan O. Hatch and Mark A. Noll. Oxford University Press, Inc. Copyright 1982. Page 86.*

Continental Congress) gave birth to the most powerful and bountiful Country in the World; and in September 17, 1787, created almost the most perfect Constitution of all times; yes, this Great Nation, America, is always capable of restoring and rereforming its Reformation of the sixteenth century, and performing thereby without much fanfare, footlights and hullabaloo, but rather spontaneously, slowly, and sternly:

First, the unification of its different and diverse sects, denominations, congregations and churches, if not into one oneness, at least into or under one single Denomination, no matter then, even with multiproliferating cells (but, dependant professionally, dogmatically, and hierarchically, on a prior-Bishop as in primeval apostleship[608] or in the image and likeness, somehow, of the 51 American States (under one sovereignty).

Second, the sainted synthesis of days of yore of Catholicism and Protestantism (Even, here too, without strict structural fusion or union).

It is only by the help of the Holy Spirit that this very unification of Protestantism and Catholicism can be achieved and accomplished.

---

[608]-*(1 Peter 2:25 and Paul 3:1)*

343

Wasn't this also the very wish of George Carey, the 103rd Archbishop of Canterbury, when in 1985 (as reports Time Magazine, August 6, 1990) he "declared that Evangelicals and Roman Catholics, though longtime adversaries, now "stand firm" together for a historic faith against the insidious bloodletting which extreme liberalism perpetrates on the body Christian?"

And to prepare for this blessing event, two fundamental factors at least are required, and using here Gorbachev's wonderful words:

First, more Glasnot or openness, on the part of Catholicism (Marriage, particularly of the clergy, should be, at least, the first step here; and that according to the Scriptures themselves.[609] As for celibacy of clergymen and clergywomen, it should be in turn according to their own will and choices, as attest here too the Scriptures themselves.[610]

Second, more Perestroika or restructuring on the part of Protestantism (By putting, for instance, a stop, rather an end, a

---

[609]-(1 Corinthians 7:9, 28, 36 and 1 Timothy 3:2 and 4:3)

[610]-(Matthew 19:12 and 1 Corinthians 7:32, 33, 37)

344

decisive end, to all its numerous congregations and diverse denominations and churches).

Cardinal O'Connor says, as reports the New York Times National Sunday, July 15, 1990, "There is no question that greater unity within Orthodoxy itself would make easier to bridge the differences between Eastern Orthodoxy, Roman Catholicism and Protestantism." Consequently, I deem, it suffices that a unified Catholic-Protestant Church woos, that the unified Orthodoxy coos, and thereby ensues naturally and automatically the crumbling of both the spiritual and iron curtains between all Christians and all Continents alike: Another, yes indeed, direct initiative of the triumphant trio Pope John Paul II, Michael Gorbachev,[611] Yeltsin, these three great men of the century.

For, concerning Russia, if Lenin has ridden the Communist current and converged it his own way, both Michael Gorbachev (no matter an overt communist or a covert Christian) and Yeltsin, backed by their great people, did ride it, in turn, but twisted, and turned back its course definitley; and to the unlikelihood of the whole world, without the

---

[611]-*Michael, in Syrian Aramaic language, means the meek or the humble of God.*

shedding of blood whatsoever, as nobody could, or dared to save by the will of God, who alone is the very maker of history.

Even though sociological factors were indeed the most fundemantal and most dominant in the collapse of communism, yet we can not deny or exclude the divine element either.

For if "All things work together for good to those who love God" as Says Saint Paul to the Romans (8:38) that means undoubtedly that it is the very creator and instigator of "all things" himself who intervened, in due time, to save from oppression, tyranny, paganisim and the like, such a good and godly peoples that are the Orthodox Russians. Didn't the Lord assert in the mouth of Haggai, "I will overthrow the throne of kingdoms. I will destroy the strength of the Gentile (or the atheists) kingdoms?"[612]

Thus again, it is, yes, Gorbachev and Yeltsin themselves, supported by their great Russian people who saved servile Russia for seven decades to atheism, fulfilling thereby Dostoyevski's prophecy, "The people will rise up against the atheist and subdue him; and unified Christian Russia will appear under the

---

[612]-(Haggai 2:22)

Orthodox Church. . . for the Russian people are a God-bearing people."[613]

So then, praise must be raised to God again and again from Heaven and Earth simultaneously,

"Glory to God in the Highest
And on Earth peace, good will
toward men!"

And the final question here,

"Who are the sole competent in the American Protestant Church, who can perform this "other" great miracle (comparing it with that of Gorbachev and Yeltsin) by the help of the Holy Spirit", namely, this Sainted Synthesis of bygone days of Protestantism and Catholicism?

The response is:

The very, truly pure, zealous, courageous namely the elite who can come, and claim with Paul, "called to be apostle of Jesus Christ

---

[613]-*The Brothers Karamazov-Translated by Andrew N. MacAndrew. Bantam Books. Copyright 1981. Page 380.*

through the will of God"[614] and, "appointed a preacher, and apostle, and teacher" of his gospel."[615]

So that we all:

-Maybe "One as the Father, the Son, and the Holy Spirit are."[616]

-May keep "The unity of the Spirit in the Bond of peace. There is one body and one Spirit, just as you were called in one hope of your calling;
One Lord, One faith, one baptism;

One God and Father of all, who is above all, and through all, and in you all."[617]

-May in the likeness of "heavenly Jerusalem."[618] have "One holy, Catholic and Apostolic Church," as professes the Niceno-Constantinopolitan creed.

---

[614]-*(1 Corinthians 1:1)*

[615]-*(2 Timothy 1:11)*

[616]-*(Matt 28:19, John 17:1, I John 5:7)*

[617]-*(Ephesians 4:3-6)*

[618]-*(Heb 12:22)*

I BELIEVE in one God, the Father, the Almighty Creator of heaven and earth, and of all things visible and invisible.

And in one Lord, Jesus Christ, the only-begotten Son of God, begotten of the Father before all ages, Light of Light, true God of true God, begotten, not created, of one essence with the Father, through whom all things were made; who for us and for our salvation came down from heaven and was incarnate of the Holy Spirit and the Virgin Mary and became human; who was crucified for us under Pontius Pilate, and suffered and was buried; who rose on the third day, according to the Scriptures, and ascended into heaven and is seated at the right hand of the Father; and who is coming again with glory to judge the living and the dead; and his kingdom will have no end.

And in the Holy Spirit, the Lord, the Giver of Life, who proceeds from the Father, who together with the Father and the Son is worshiped and glorified, who spoke through the prophets.

In one, holy, catholic, and apostolic Church.

I acknowledge one baptism for the forgiveness of sins.

I look for the resurrection of the dead, and the life of the age to come. Amen.